CREATING LIVES OF
BOUNDLESS PROMISE

GOD WRITES A BETTER STORY

BRUCE MAIN

God Writes A Better Story: Creating Lives of Boundless Promise
Bruce D. Main

Copyright © 2024 by Bruce D. Main

Published by The Core Media Group, Inc., www.thecoremediagroup.com.
The author is represented by WordServe Literary Group, Ltd., www.wordserveliterary.com.

Cover Design: William Butler
Interior Design: Nadia Guy

ISBN 978-1-950465-33-0

All rights reserved. No part of this publication may be reproduced, stored in a retrieval system, or transmitted in any form or by any means—electronic, mechanical, photocopy, recording, scanning, or other—except for brief quotation in printed reviews, without the prior written permission of the publisher.

Unless otherwise noted, Scriptures quotations are taken from The Holy Bible, New International Version®, NIV®, Copyright © 1973, 1978, 1984, 2011 by Biblica, Inc.® Used by permission. All rights reserved worldwide.

Scripture marked PHILLIPS are taken from The New Testament in Modern English by J.B Phillips copyright © 1960, 1972 J. B. Phillips. Administered by The Archbishops' Council of the Church of England. Used by Permission.

Scripture quotations marked MSG are taken from THE MESSAGE, copyright © 1993, 2002, 2018 by Eugene H. Peterson. Used by permission of NavPress. All rights reserved. Represented by Tyndale House Publishers, Inc.

Printed in the United States of America.

TABLE OF CONTENTS

Day One: A Better Story...Not A Perfect One | **07**
Day Two: Made to Flourish | **11**
Day Three: Go Deep | **15**
Day Four: Growing Wings | **21**
Day Five: Paradox of Pain | **25**
Day Six: Eyes of Artists | **29**
Day Seven: Which House? | **33**
Day Eight: Cursing God | **37**
Day Nine: Givers & Takers | **41**
Day Ten: Ordinary Heroes | **45**

Day Eleven: Last Words | **49**
Day Twelve: Sow what? | **53**
Day Thirteen: Zip Code Burden | **57**
Day Fourteen: Second Mile Vacancy | **61**
Day Fifteen: Aching Visionaries | **65**
Day Sixteen: Shattered Dreams | **69**
Day Seventeen: Why Protest? | **73**
Day Eighteen: Spurs & Burrs | **77**
Day Nineteen: Love Wastefully | **81**
Day Twenty: Not the Road | **85**

Day Twenty-One: What's in Your Hand? | **89**
Day Twenty-Two: Secret of Contentment | **93**
Day Twenty-Three: Power of Purpose | **99**
Day Twenty-Four: Sacred Scars | **103**
Day Twenty-Five: Passionate Patience | **107**
Day Twenty-Six: Which Parade? | **111**
Day Twenty-Seven: The Futility of Hate | **115**
Day Twenty-Eight: Stretching | **119**
Day Twenty-Nine: Where Are the Oaks? | **123**
Day Thirty: Gratitude Journals | **127**

Day Thirty-One: Is Social Justice Biblical? | **131**
Day Thirty-Two: Beautiful Moments | **137**
Day Thirty-Three: Saints in Our Midst | **141**
Day Thirty-Four: Habit of Hope | **145**
Day Thirty-Five: A Few Good Bricks | **151**
Day Thirty-Six: Open Table | **155**
Day Thirty-Seven: Thanksgiving Calls | **159**
Day Thirty-Eight: Angels Eat Granola Bars | **163**
Day Thirty-Nine: She Said Yes | **167**
Day Forty: Flowers in Barren Places | **171**

Grateful for all our volunteers, board members, donors, staff, fellows and youth who have committed their lives to writing and living the better story.

DAY ONE
A BETTER STORY...NOT A PERFECT ONE

"We run these stories over and over again like hamsters on a wheel; we go nowhere in our inner life development..." [1]
–Angel Kyodo Williams

"I now realize that God writes a *better story than I do*," confessed James to the group.

Sitting in the room were some of the most remarkable people I've ever known—founders and directors of our inner-city programs, schools and start up NGO's in Africa. I considered all of them remarkable because they had all forfeited personal gain to serve some of the poorest and most challenging communities in the world—Camden, Trenton, North Little Rock, under-resourced communities in Uganda and rural outposts in Malawi. Remarkable because these individuals step out in faith each day to address the most pressing social issues facing disenfranchised youth. Remarkable because they dream big and are building organizations from meager resources.

"James," I questioned. "What do you mean God writes a better story than you?"

"Here's the story I wanted to write for the kids I work with in my city," James disclosed with a chuckle. "I want my students to graduate from high school and go to college. When they graduate, I would love to see them get a good job, get married, have a few kids and donate to our ministry. That's the story I hope to write."

"What's the matter with that story?" I mumbled to myself. Considering the odds stacked against kids growing up in these communities, I thought his hopeful vision made for an amazing story. After all, dropout rates from our local schools are well above national averages. Many kids never attend a college or university. Some sociologists and criminologists argue that odds are higher for a kid from our community to go to jail than college. In countries like Malawi, less than one percent of the population will ever attain a university degree. Against that backdrop, James' story sounded peculiarly optimistic to me. Program evaluators would like his story. Benefactors would love the story. Board members would feel confident that we were fulfilling our mission if successful stories like the one James hoped for his youth became the norm.

"But there was this kid," continued James. "I'd invested a lot of time in his life. Mentoring. Tutoring. Going to the movies. Ice cream!"

Then along came the local drug dealer. The quick money was too enticing. The temptation to get rich was overpowering. Jevonny got caught in the mix.

Jevonny was picked up in a city-wide drug sweep and given a six-year sentence. "It broke my heart," lamented James.

By this time everyone in the group was hanging on to James' words. Every leader could relate. We'd all had a Jevonny in our program, we'd all had a kid (at least one) who had gotten swept into the violence and drug culture of the streets, we'd all had kids go to prison who should have gone to college and succeeded.

Six years passed. James sent letters and made the occasional visit.

"When Jevonny got out of jail I was one of the first people he called," continued James. "He told me a moment in prison that changed his life."

Jevonny shared about one particular night he was restless and couldn't sleep. Lying on his bunk, looking up at the ceiling, he asked himself where he had experienced the most love in his life. Hands down, it was with James and his team. Then he asked himself what James and his team had in common. It was simple: they were Christians and serious about living out their faith. "So, I became a Christian in prison and started attending a Bible study," confided Jevonny to James. "I also learned to cut hair. I went to barber school."

"That story made my day," continued James. "I was overjoyed." But the story got better.

"I'm wondering if I can set up a barber shop in your living room on Friday nights," Jevonny asked. "I'd like to start cutting hair for the drug dealers in the community—especially their kids."

At that point James looked at our group of leaders sitting on the edge of their chairs. "So guess what?" chuckled James, "Every Friday night Jevonny is cutting hair in my living room, sharing God's love and grace with the guys with whom he used to sell drugs."

"Now that's a story I *never* could have written," gushed James. "I've come to the conclusion that *God writes better stories.* Better stories than we can even imagine."

For the next month I couldn't shake James' line: "God writes a better story." It resonated deeply with me. It was the sermon I needed to hear at that moment.

I meditated on those words. I pondered their truth. I shared the story with other friends who were going through challenging times. I shared it with some wealthy parents whose kid had gotten involved with the wrong crowd. I shared it with minister friend who was going through their own difficult and dark time. I shared it with friends whose lives weren't turning out the way they had planned. And in each situation, I found that Jevonny's story brought them hope.

James' story that day was an important reminder—a reminder that the paths of our lives take twists and turns. Bad things happen. People betray and disappoint one another. Marriages fall apart. Health fails. We have moral lapses, get caught in ruts and find ourselves heading down paths that rob our energy and steal our vision. We wake up one day and wonder how the last decade vanished so quickly.

But all these situations can become part of a better story God wants to write with our lives. We don't need to throw in the towel or settle for mediocrity. God redeems our pain, heals our relationships, guides our footsteps, challenges our limited visions, prompts us to take risks…and helps us write a *better* story—one we could never imagine ourselves.

REFLECTION

> "Christians tell the story of the God who created the world and called it good, and who calls human beings to live into a vision of abundant life for all, where no one will hurt or be destroyed…as co-creators, human beings are characters within God's story but also coauthors with God, helping determine what happens next, working alongside the Spirit to shape the world. Made in God's image, they are called to help God finish the holy work of creation."[2]
>
> –Meredith Dodd

WRITING THE BETTER STORY

1. What was/is your dream for your life?
2. In what ways are you co-writing your story with God?
3. Can you imagine a "better story" for your life? If so, what might it look like?

DAY TWO
MADE TO FLOURISH

> *"We are created out of love and are made to energize the world in love. Aging can be either a life of nostalgia or a wholehearted engagement with the future."* [3]
> –Ilia Delio

That early Church Father, Iraneous of Lyons, said it best: "The glory of God is the human person *fully* alive." A human being, fully alive, is the ultimate gift to God.

Imagine if we really believed, lived, and acted on Iraneous' charge. Imagine if we wrestled with the question: *what does it really mean to be fully alive?* According to Iraneous, bringing God glory is more important than getting "saved," living up to some moral code, or getting ready for eternity in heaven. It's more than showing up to church, tithing big sums of money and memorizing Bible verses. Anybody can play that game and never experience a kind of abundant life that moves them to a place of being fully alive.

As the old itinerate preacher, Billy Sunday, used to say, most people have "…got just enough religion to make them miserable." There are lots of miserable Christians populating the world—Christians who have substituted a kind of role-playing religious charade for a vibrant form of abundant life. Authentic faith means the ability to live life more fully and more courageously, always growing into God's larger vision for our lives. The status quo is at odds with a dynamic and creative God.

God's intent for every human being is for us to live into our unique fullness—a fullness of purpose, a fullness of intellect, a fullness of health, a fullness of vision, and a fullness of mission. This looks and means something different for each of us. My life, *fully alive*, will look different from your fully alive life. I'm not Nelson Mandela, Abraham Lincoln or Mother Teresa. I'll never match Albert Einstein's intellectual capacity, nor the athletic prowess of LeBron James. Bill Gates is an entrepreneurial genius who is beyond most of us. My siblings are completely different human beings than I am. Let's stop comparing. Every person is unique. Our uniqueness leads to the creation of our own story—a story that will be different than our friends, our colleagues and our family members.

My father loved accounting. Numbers and balance sheets were his thing. Dad would have been thrilled to have me follow in his footsteps, but I can hardly balance my checkbook. I love risk. I love coloring outside the lines. I'm an entrepreneur who is always looking to create something new. Details and spreadsheets are like another language. It wasn't the path for me. I, too, was called to embrace my uniqueness and live into the fullness of who I was created to be.

I love to reminisce about my first car out of college—a classic 1966 Volkswagen Beetle. I paid $300 for it, with 19,000 original miles on the odometer. Even for a graduate student, it was quite a deal. The car ran for 10 years—even though I would occasionally have to coast down a hill and pop the clutch to get it started. But a VW Bug is still a VW Bug. It's not a Porsche. Not a Mercedes. Not a Land Rover. Not a BMW. It's VW Bug that transported me through graduate school, accompanied me through a courtship with my wife, and traveled Route 66 from Los Angeles to New Jersey on my honeymoon. I loved that car.

Eventually a gasket cracked, and I had to make the big decision—would I invest $1,500 into a 25-year-old car, or would I leave it parked at the end of my driveway, procrastinating its migration to the scrap yard? Newly married, and barely able to afford diapers for our newborn, my bargaining position to refurnish my vintage car had little leverage. In retrospect, I wish I had held onto the car until our financial situation improved. But a neighbor offered me $300 (what paid for the car) to tow it out of my driveway. I took the offer, stocked up on diapers and put the balance in my savings account. For a few months I waxed and waned with nostalgia. After 5 months I had forgotten all about it.

Six months later I saw a VW Beetle parked in front of my neighbor's house. Surely it couldn't be mine? The shiny cherry red paint job sparkled in the afternoon sun, the new chrome bumpers almost blinded me, and fancy hubcaps could have doubled as dinner plates. Beautiful. Stunning. I walked closer to the vehicle and could not believe my eyes. It was my car! Fully restored. Yet even with all the sparkle and glimmer, it was still a VW Bug—just a better version of its former self.

That's the kind of story God wants to write with us. God takes our unique, one-of-a-kind lives, and wants to write something extraordinary with them.

REFLECTION:

> "Don't ask what the world needs. Ask what makes you come alive and go do it. Because what the world needs is people who have come alive."
> —Howard Thurman
>
> "I was a middle-aged lady, set in my ways, when I decided to be baptized. And when that water poured over my head, I realized the big problem with my new religion: God actually lives in other people. I couldn't be a Christian by myself. I couldn't choose who was my brother and sister...that's a really different story from the one that's sold to us every day, which insists each one of us is individually responsible for managing our own economic and political salvation." [4]
> —Sara Miles, Director of Ministry St. Gregory of Nyssa Episcopal Church

WRITING THE BETTER STORY:

1. Take a short inventory of your life. Are there moments you would rather forget? Dismiss? Erase? How might you own these parts of your story? How might they be redeemed to become instrumental in helping others to heal?

2. How might you call forth another person's God story? Write down the names of a few of people you know: can you be more intentional in seeing their beauty, affirming their gifts, and encouraging their sacredness?

DAY THREE
GO DEEP

"Put out into deep water and let down the nets for a catch."
–Luke 5:4

Gerry Rice leaned across the table, cleared her throat, and whispered, "What do you actually *do* on the social justice committee?"

It was the annual church pot-luck luncheon and Gerry decided to make conversation. She didn't typically attend these events, but for some reason that day she was corralled into eating a chicken salad sandwich and a plate of potato salad. Gerry glanced at her wristwatch, remembering she had a music recital later that afternoon.

Gerry plays the viola professionally, teaching at the prestigious Curtis Institute of Music in Philadelphia, and plays for the Philadelphia Pops—she's not the professional football player who made gravity-defying Super Bowl winning catches for the San Francisco 49ers.

"Well....we...talk about issues of justice," stammered the gentleman, evidently caught off guard by the directness of the question. "You know, things like immigration, racism and poverty."

"Would you be interested in feeding children?" retorted Gerry.

"Well, that does sound rather intriguing," replied the gentleman. "What are you thinking?"

Gerry shared how her brother-in-law was associated with an organization called Feed My Starving Children. The organization mobilizes volunteers to package small bags of high-protein meals for starving children around the world. The following week there would be a regional packing event in Clinton, NJ.

"Why don't you go check them out?" requested the man. "Come back and tell us if it's an organization worth partnering with."

That's all Gerry needed. She was off and running. The next week she found herself in a church basement with 60 volunteers filling zip lock bags with rice and dried beans. That visit birthed a vision.

"I started crying," she confessed. "At one point I looked down at my hands and realized they were saving lives."

Gerry came back to her church, met with the social justice committee and shared her excitement about mobilizing her town to pack meals. Then she encountered her first obstacle: the committee had no money. Next, she went to the senior pastor. "There's no money in the budget," she was told. Then in the next session she was asked, "How are you going to raise the money?"

"I honestly didn't know how I could make it happen," she shared. "All I know is that I felt called to do it."

It was at that moment Gerry had to decide if she would get off the beach and move into deep waters. Would she let go of the security of wading close to the shore and venture into an unfamiliar place? With no experience raising money, Gerry would have to believe that God would come alongside her.

"Mother Teresa has a great quote," Gerry reminded me one day over coffee. "God doesn't choose the qualified. God qualifies those God chooses." You know you're going deep when you start quoting Mother Teresa.

In 2013, Gerry and her volunteers raised enough money to pack 22,000 meals. In 2014, her growing volunteers packaged 50,000 meals—and in 2015 that number quadrupled to 200,000 meals. This past year over 1,000 volunteers assembled in the local Jr. high school gym over 3 days and packaged 500,000 meals. People from every walk of life show up to pack—different races, different religions and different ages. Gerry's vision not only saves lives, but it is saving the soul of her community.

"How are you different?" I asked her recently. *"How has this changed you?"*

Gerry paused and looked me in the eye, "My 'wants' are so different than they were 5 years ago."

This is what happens when people venture into the deep waters. God begins to write a new story—a story of adventure, of risk, of transformation.

Let's be honest. Most of us would rather live on the beach. Maybe dangle our toes in the water. Going deep means letting go, losing control, and putting our trust in something other than ourselves. Deep water is a frightening place because we have to pry our fingers away from the things that make us feel safe.

But it's in the deep waters where we find the opportunity to experience the abundance of God in ways that we could never experience by staying the shore. This is not just about material abundance. It's an abundance of wisdom, faith, and inner peace.

In Luke, Peter and his band of fisherman experienced abundance. Notice their response after the catch. They call over the other boat and share their fish—because the boat is beginning to sink (5:6). What does that say about what we should do with God's provision? God's abundance, God's blessing—if not shared—ultimately sinks us. Too much of a good thing is never meant to be kept for oneself.

Here's the part of the story I really find revealing. When Simon experiences the best fishing day of his career he is overcome with its insignificance. Simon wants to go even deeper. Deep down, Simon has encountered the mystery and goodness of God. Simon wants *more*, and he's willing to leave everything to follow this man Jesus. In economic terms, the decision is absurd. Peter's fishing company has just hit the fishing lottery. For the first time in months, the balance sheet is positive. Employees have received bonuses. The banks are happy and have extended his line of credit. Shares in the company have seen record one-day gains.

Simon has experienced a radical transformation. Even his name will change to Peter—derived from the Greek word for "Rock." And it's on the shoulders of this unlikely fisherman that the Christian movement begins. It's quite a story, isn't it? It all begins with a choice to go deep.

REFLECTION

> "Piety is openness to the unmanipulated mystery of life… those who wish to see the living God and truly follow Christ must have the courage to learn to swim in deep waters, not in the shallows. God is in the depths; God is not to be found in the shallows." [5]
>
> —Tomas Halike
>
> "Start by doing what's necessary; then do what's possible; and suddenly you are doing the impossible."
>
> —St. Francis of Assisi

WRITING THE BETTER STORY

1. In what areas of your life do you need to go deeper? Practically, what might that look like?

2. What are the fears that hold you back from stepping off "the beach" and going to a deeper place?

3. Take a step off the beach this week. Come back next week and write a little about the experience. How did you grow?

DAY FOUR
GROWING WINGS

> *"By faith Abraham, when called to go to a place he would later receive as his inheritance, obeyed and went, even though he did not know where he was going."*
> –Hebrews 11:8

This past Sunday the pastor introduced his sermon by asking the congregation if they remembered a day when they had a significant spiritual experience. Friday, April 3rd, 2020 popped into my mind. It's a day I'll not forget—perhaps my most significant spiritual moment during the pandemic.

At 1 p.m. that day, I had the privilege of telling our staff that we would not lay off anyone, that we would continue to show up for our children and we would plan and prepare for a post-Coronavirus Camden. In short—I told the team we were staying together and staying the course. I'll admit, I was a little nervous leading up to that moment. Once I shared those words, I knew there was no turning back. Verbally making a promise to support the livelihood of 60+ employees, their families and hundreds of youths was a daunting promise. Yet once the words were uttered I felt a sense of liberation. Commitment works that way—this commitment would define the future of UrbanPromise.

Making this promise may not seem like a big deal, but let me share some context. Our accounts closed in March 2020 with a 50% shortfall in revenue, we had 3 weeks of cash in the bank, the stock market was in a freefall and our three fourth-quarter fundraisers needed to be cancelled—events which typically generate a significant percentage of our annual budget. *Economically vulnerable* would accurately describe our organizational situation.

Some might argue that it was irresponsible to make this kind of announcement to our staff. And looking through a certain lens, they would be absolutely correct. If we based our decision on cash flow projections, the stock market, unemployment numbers and an uncertain economic forecast, that's a winning argument.

But we call ourselves a "faith-based" organization. I often remind our team that "faith-based" has less to do with our doctrine and more to do with how we act as God's people. Faith is a verb. Actions speak louder than words. So what does it mean to act in faith during those moments when common sense and a shaky economic forecast suggest a more conservative path forward? At this particular moment being "faith-based" meant taking the proverbial leap of faith. Or as the late theologian William Sloan Coffin used to quip: "Jump first, then grow wings."

I've come to believe that taking a leap of faith is often a critical first step to create conditions for the miraculous to happen. It's difficult to put into words. But faith is more than an intellectual assent to a set of propositional truths. Faith is *action*. Faith is committing beyond our human capabilities and placing ourselves in a vulnerable space…and hoping that God shows up.

Speaking of God and faith, I have a favorite quote I've returned to over the years—somewhat reluctantly, I'll admit. The source slips my mind, but the words I've not forgotten: *"Faith is putting ourselves in situations where, if God doesn't show up, we're in trouble."*

Those familiar with the scriptures probably recognize that this quote is rooted in an observable and repeated pattern: page after page, the Bible records stories about ordinary people who put themselves in situations where…if God doesn't show up…they're in trouble.

There's Moses. Waist deep in the Red Sea with Pharaoh's army closing in…God needs to show up. Then there's this young boy named David up against this rather large giant named Goliath…God needs to show up. There's Gideon. Joseph in the Egyptian jail. The young men who took a stand against an egotistical king name Nebuchadnezzar and found themselves in a fiery furnace. The widow who gave all her resources. The disciples who respond to the simple words, "Follow me."

An active faith places these characters in situations where God needs to show up…or they are in trouble.

Four years have passed since I first made that announcement to the staff. Since then, as a community we have experienced the miraculous. God has shown up. We've made payroll every week. Our donors and partners have responded with humbling generosity and sacrifice. Programs have continued—although they have taken new forms. Most importantly, the faith of our people has been deepened as we've supported, encouraged, and ministered to one another, our youth, and our families. Something powerful happened. It all began with a decision to go to a place where if God "didn't show up, we'd be in trouble."

Einstein put it best: "There are two ways to live: you can live as if nothing is a miracle; you can live as if everything is a miracle." I'm choosing the latter.

REFLECTIONS

"Jesus praises faith even more than love. 'Your faith has saved you' is often his concluding word (for example, Luke 8:48). Why? Because typically, wisdom, love or further growth will not go deeper without another opening up or letting go. For some reason, each time you have to learn it again and 'reopen.' Faith enlightens the path behind you, but as a rule, in front of you it is still dark. Now, however, not so threatening or impossible, because for you 'a light shines on in the darkness, and the darkness cannot overpower it." (John 1:5)[6]

—Richard Rohr

"Abraham was not a conventional leader. He did not rule a nation…but he was a role model of leadership as Judaism understands it. He took responsibility. He acted; he did not wait for others to act."[7]

—Rabbi Jonathan Sacks

"I love the recklessness of faith; first you jump, and then you grow wings."[8]

—William Sloane Coffin

WRITING THE BETTER STORY

1. When is the last time you really "jumped" before growing wings? What was the result?
2. Is God calling you to step out in faith? If so, what do you think God is calling you to do?
3. What would you do if you weren't afraid?

DAY FIVE
PARADOX OF PAIN

"To love someone is to reveal to them their capabilities for life, the light that is shining in them."
–Jean Vanier

A beautifully wrapped box leaned against my office door. Whoever left it there had taken great care to neatly fold the paper, ensuring exact creases and flush corners. A complimentary silver bow juxtaposes the black paper, announcing a certain level of quality. This was no Dollar Store gift—maybe Bed, Bath and Beyond.

What struck me was the unusual weight of the parcel as I hoisted it to my hip. Alabaster bookends? Paper weights? A stone carving of some sorts? It was heavy. Really heavy.

I opened the card first, tearing a small hole and sliding my index finger along the top. As I pulled the card from its holster, a neatly folded piece of paper fell to the floor. I picked it up and read:

"Principles of Embalming—final grade, A-minus." I looked again, double checking the document. "Funeral Service Pathology—final grade, A." Evidently, I was viewing a transcript. No ordinary transcript. A transcript for funeral directing. Funeral directing?

"Dear Bruce," began the note. "This ministry made a difference for me, once again, so I could finish the spring semester. Your gift didn't just encourage me to finish the semester, but it reminded me that I can do all things through Christ who gives me strength. Love, Chivon."

For a moment I pondered. I'd known Chivon since she was a teenager. She sang in our gospel choir. She served as a teen leader and taught in our day camps. Suddenly I remembered her SOS email one cold morning six months earlier. Chivon had run out of money and needed $300 to stay enrolled in her funeral services degree program. A few of us scraped together the money. Apparently, it made the difference. Not only did she finish the degree, but it reminded her of God's faithfulness and gave her the confidence to believe that her life could be extraordinary.

But I was curious. What propels a young woman—with two undergraduate degrees—to aspire to be a funeral director? I picked up the phone.

"Remind me again, why are you becoming a mortician?" I naively asked her. "In 32 years of working with Camden students, you'll be the first."

"When my grandmother died, I didn't have money to pay to get her hair done," she reminisced. "So, I asked the funeral parlor. They let me do it. I had a few hours with my grandmother. It was a chance to grieve. A chance to talk with her. A chance to relive memories. When the funeral came, I didn't fall apart."

Chivon shared that her time with her deceased grandmother got her thinking about the opportunities and stresses around the death of loved ones—especially in her community. There are sacred opportunities to grieve with people, listen, pray and comfort. And there are stresses when families don't have the resources to buy a coffin or hold a funeral. Many families have no life insurance. Many live paycheck to paycheck. A funeral can put a family in debt. Chivon wanted to make a difference in this unusual industry.

Extraordinary lives don't happen by accident. They are often the result of choices and experiences. Some are strategic. Sometimes it involves doing the right thing at the right moment. Sometimes it means just being in the right place at the right time, prepared and ready to take advantage of the fleeting opportunity that drops in a person's lap. For Chivon, her calling was discovered in her pain. In her loss, her heart opened to new possibilities.

Today Chivon works in the funeral services industry. Because of her own experience of suffering and loss, Chivon has become more aware of people's needs—and she acted on that awareness. Her colleagues praise her empathy and care for grieving families. Bishop Tutu of South Africa put it poignantly when he said, "Suffering can of course embitter the one who suffers. But in many other circumstances, it can ennoble the sufferer."[9] Chivon has been ennobled. "I used to be embarrassed and ashamed of my story," concluded Chivon. "Now I realize it's my unique story and it can be used to gift hope and strength to others."

Those neatly wrapped parcels outside my door? Three beautiful scented candles. I will keep them until the wax disappears—reminders of the light we all possess and our individual capacity to bring healing to our world. Reflect the light. Let it shine.

REFLECTIONS

> "Each one of us, and every action we make, has a quality of aliveness to it, a fragrance or vibrancy uniquely its own. If the outer form of who we are in this life is conveyed by our physical bodies, the inner form—our real beauty and authenticity—is conveyed in the quality of our aliveness. This is where the secret of our being lies...Jesus taught 'the Kingdom of Heaven is within you' (Luke 17:21)...to realize the Kingdom of Heaven here and now...is really a matter of developing a kind of X-ray vision that can look right through the physical appearance of things and respond directly to their innermost aliveness and quality."[10]
>
> –Cynthia Bourgeault

"Find your story. Know your story. Remember your story. Tell your story. And always know, that at the end of your story, you are its hero."[11]

—Father Greg Boyle

WRITING THE BETTER STORY

1. Think of some painful moments in your life-write them down.

2. How has God used your pain to expand your empathy and compassion? Are there ways for your painful life moments open new doors to bring healing to others?

DAY SIX
EYES OF ARTISTS

"To pray means to open one's eyes and watch what is happening, what is coming, the dangers and the opportunities."
–Jurgen Moltmann

My son had a chance to spend a semester abroad his junior year of college—in Florence, Italy. While I was in college, studying abroad meant going to the library and looking at National Geographic Magazines. Times have changed. Four years on one campus hardly qualifies for an "enlightened" education anymore. My son Calvin, on the other hand, went to Florence. On weekends he would take the train to Rome to tour the Vatican, hitch a ride to Milan to visit famous cathedrals or eat pasta in quaint villages in Tuscany. I'll admit, I was a little jealous. As his semester concluded, I decided to invade Calvin's space and join his adventure. I booked my flight to Florence.

Walking into the *Galleria dell'Accademia* for the first time took my breath away. Inside the entryway, standing 17 feet tall, is one of the greatest sculptures of the Renaissance period—six tons of Tuscany marble chiseled into an awe-inspiring depiction of the boy David. Cradled over his left shoulder is a sling, clutched in his right hand a rock—the shepherd is ready to confront Goliath. Larger than life in proportion, this vision of youthful strength and prowess was a radical departure from other artistic depictions of biblical heroes. I could have spent the whole afternoon just sitting in its presence. Then I read the story about how this piece of art was conceived.

Agostino di Duccio was the first artist to take a crack at the slab of marble. According to legend, he saw some imperfections in the massive stone, feared his reputation would be ruined if he tried using a chisel, and walked away from the project. Abandoned for 10 years in a junkyard, Antonio Rossellino was the next to try to carve it. Rossellino found the stone too difficult and gave up. Another 30 years passed before the upstart artist, Michaelangelo, saw something in the stone and began to release the beauty it possessed. Michaelangelo worked freehand. No plaster models, no sketches, no practice miniatures. He just saw the image in the stone and "released" it. Unbelievable. *Genius*.

Finally completed in 1504, Michaelangelo's *David* has become a central fixture in the Florentine artistic landscape and cemented him as one of the greatest sculptors to walk the earth. Sixteenth-century Italian painter Giorgio Vasari wrote, "Whoever has seen this work need not trouble to see any other work executed in sculpture, either in our own or in other times."

Michaelangelo had the ability to see beyond the imperfections, beyond the flaws, and beyond the idiosyncrasies of that particular piece of marble. Buried deep within the rock, Angelo saw an image of greatness and beauty—a story that needed to be released from its captivity. In fact, Michaelangelo is noted to have said about another piece of art: "I saw the angel in the marble and carved until I set him free."

That's what great artists do, isn't it? Their eyes release the ordinary from the captivity of the mundane and display it for the world to see. That's what God wants to do with our lives. Encrusted in social expectations, fears, and cultural driven visions for our lives, like a master artist, God wants to chip away everything that diminishes the potential of our lives. From the flaws and brokenness of our past, God wants to call forth our truest and greatest self.

The Artistic Eye of Jesus

When I ponder Jesus' earthly ministry, I find a man who looked upon people with "artistic" eyes. Beyond the imperfections, flaws, ailments, and societal prejudices, Jesus could see into the hearts of people and called forth their greatness. His vision for every human life was wholeness, abundance, and purpose. His vision for those he touched was to breathe new life into their story and equip them with the tools to write a better story.

Jesus could have seen an impetuous, cowardly, uneducated fisherman named Peter. Instead, he saw a man on whom he built his church. Peter's life became a story few could have ever imagined—yet we're still impacted by his life today.

Jesus could have seen a man with a contagious disease, someone to be avoided at all costs. Instead, he sees a leper who could be healed and who become a testimony of God's grace, compassion and healing power. After his healing, his story changed. Who knows how many lives this leper impacted as he left the fringes of society and reintegrated into his community!

Jesus could have seen a lying, cheating, self-promoting government collaborator named Zacheus. Instead, he saw a man who could model repentance and contrition. Can you imagine the jaw-dropping reactions of those who were paid back from being swindled out of their hard-earned money? What a story!

When Jesus is anointed with oil by a woman, it could have tarnished his reputation as a holy man. Instead, he saw a woman who has the capacity to display extravagant love. And it was this unnamed woman who was upheld as an example of lavish love for perpetuity.

When Jesus encountered a man with an evil spirit (Mark 1:21-28), we could argue with the scholars as to whether he was demon possessed or suffering from a kind of psychological disorder. But when we venture down that rabbit trail, we miss the bigger truth. The bottom line is that the possessed man was not flourishing as a human being. His life story had hit a tragic road bump, limiting him from becoming all God created him to be. So Jesus saw beyond his condition; the condition stripping the man of his dignity and life at its fullest—and he calls it out of him: "Be silent! Come out!"

Once liberated, God begins to write a new story with the man…a story he could never have imagined or written himself. His former condition became a part of his testimony. He did not have to be embarrassed or sweep the truth under the rug. That painful, difficult chapter became a reference point for God's capacity to redeem a life.

REFLECTION

"You never have to prove yourself. God's love doesn't seek value; it creates it. It's not because we have value that we are loved, but because we're love that we have value. So you don't have to prove yourself ever. That's taken care of."[12]
–William Sloane Coffin

"Jesus says, 'You are the light of the world.' I like even more what Jesus doesn't say. He does not say, 'One day, if you are more perfect and try really hard, you'll be light.' He doesn't say 'If you play by the rules, cross your T's and dot your I's, then maybe you'll become light.' No. He says, straight out, 'You are light.' It is the truth of who you are, waiting only for you to discover it."[13]
–Father Greg Boyle

WRITING THE BETTER STORY

1. What are some personal imperfections that keep you from believing that God can write a better story with your life?

2. What are some ways you can begin to look at others with the eyes of an artist?

DAY SEVEN
WHICH HOUSE?

> *"Fear hollows out our insides and secretly gnaws and eats away all the ties that bind a person to God and others."* [14]
> –Dietrich Bonhoeffer

After a long day I'll sometimes lay my head on the pillow with the hope of falling asleep quickly—instead, my restless brain begins to manufacture worst-case scenarios in the form of "what if" questions…perhaps you do the same. What if the donations stop coming in? What if the staff get tired and morale wanes? What if the current protests and cries for justice don't translate into substantial change? The what-if questions tend to make us anxious, nervous and fear-filled people.

"Fear is like a tyrant that possesses us and forces us to live in the house of fear," wrote the late Catholic theologian Henri Nouwan. "The great spiritual quest of our lives is moving from the house of fear to the house of love." [15]

Nouwan penned these words in the early 1980s at the height of the Cold War in a short and unassuming little book called *Lifesigns*. Fear of a nuclear holocaust was real in our country. Suspicion towards those in communist bloc countries soared to record highs.

So Nouwan asked the ultimate question: How do we know in which house we dwell? Do we live in the House of Fear, or do we dwell in the House of Love? His answer: the questions we ask ourselves and others reveal the house in which we dwell. Questions? Yes, any question pertaining to the preservation of power, prestige, control, or privilege is a question born in the House of Fear. The pursuit of our questions ultimately demands our time, our energy, and our resources—that's why we need to pay attention to the questions we seek to answer.

According to Nouwan, Jesus only answers three questions directly—of the 183 asked in the four Gospels. Most questions asked to Jesus come from the House or Fear: "Who will be the greatest?" "How many times must I forgive?" "By whose authority do you act?"

Jesus never bites the bait of fear-based questions. He either remains silent, volleys with another question, or answers with a story—as in the Good Samaritan (the man who sought to justify himself by asking: *who is my neighbor?*). Is Jesus rude for not answering? No. Just wise. He knows fear never gives birth to love. Fear-based questions can't be answered with love-based solutions. Jesus changes the conversation.

Now don't get me wrong, fear is real. From the smallest organism to the most complex mammal, when people are threatened, we react in fear—our reactive fear is critical for survival. But there is a difference between fear as a *warning* and *becoming* our fears—or living our fears. "Fear hollows out our inside," wrote Bonhoeffer, "and secretly gnaws and eats away all the ties that bind a person to God and others." Unchecked, unmitigated fear is destructive. Racism, bigotry, greed, violence all have their roots in fear.

Neurologically we know that the capacity of the brain is limited when fear dominates. Fear-based solutions are simplistic, reactionary, binary and often irrational. Love-based solutions are creative, patient, imaginative and appreciate the complexity of problems. This is why we need to be wary of leaders who perpetuate fear, prey on fear and offer simplistic solutions to complex problems.

"There is no fear in love," writes John in one of my favorite Bible verses, 1 John 4:18. "Fear has to do with punishment. The one who fears is not made perfect in love."

Day Seven: Which House?

Thirty-seven years ago, a group of Christians cast a vision to start a youth ministry in what was deemed the poorest and most violent city in America. We heard a lot of questions and solutions from the House of Fear. Questions about safety, insurance policies, "worthwhile" investments of time and resources. Fortunately, our founders said no to the House of Fear, pushed forward and started UrbanPromise by gathering a diverse community of people together around a common vision: Rich and poor, black and white, Latino and Asian, suburban and urban, Republican, Democrats and Independents all joined together to make a difference.

We put our fears aside and united our hearts around a vision of hope and love. Over the decades' abandoned buildings were turned into afterschool programs, boarded-up churches into wooden boat building facilities, and dilapidated row homes into high schools. We offered meaningful jobs to drug dealers, invited gang kids to join gospel choirs and turned abandoned properties into butterfly gardens. Unlikely friendships were formed across lines of race, class, and politics. Guess what? *Hope took root.* Kids enrolled in college. Alumni returned to their city as teachers, pastors, police, firefighters, and social workers. To everyone's surprise, this vision spread to 38 new locations around the world.

When people put "For Sale" signs on Houses of Fear and commit to building Houses of Love something beautiful and dynamic happens. Say no to fear and all of its ugly manifestations. Join hearts and hands with others and start building a House of Love. It's a better story. It's our only hope.

REFLECTION

> "There is no fear in love. But perfect love drives out fear because fear has to do with punishment. The one who fears is not made perfect in love."
> —1 John 4:18

"If any emotion could be named, it was fear. Fear at the unfolding horror, at what would happen if the men unleashed their anger on me...Coward is too kind a word for what I was then. What I am still."[16]

–The White Rose Resists, Amanda Barratt

WRITING THE BETTER STORY

1. What do you fear? List your fears.
2. How might you confront and lean into your fears this week? Write about the experience?
3. Write a few situations where you demonstrated courage. What can you learn from those moments?

DAY EIGHT
CURSING GOD

"Healing begins where the wound was made."
–Alice Walker

"I reached a breaking point," shared the man across the table. "I mean, I've really tried to do the right thing by God...and this is what I got in return?"

I wasn't sure how to respond. His pain started to fall from his lips: a wayward son, a tense and broken relationship with a brother, feelings of shame, anxiety about the pandemic, frustrations at work.

"I looked up the heavens and cursed God," he sputtered, tears now welling in his eyes. "I'd never done that. I couldn't believe it. I told God where to go...then just started weeping."

Something strange happened next.

"I don't know how to describe it," he continued. "Immediately I was overcome with a sense of warmth. All I can say is that I felt the presence of God. I've never felt this before. It's been weeks now. I still feel it. I know God is real. I can't explain it any other way."

Hmmm.

Within some traditions this would be known as an encounter with the "Holy Ghost". I can hear my Pentecostal friends say, "Just visit my church Sunday. This happens every week."

But my friend across the table doesn't come from that kind of religious tradition. This was new territory. Really unusual.

"It almost sounds like Paul on the Road to Damascus," I shared, stumbling for words. "Out of nowhere God shows up and turns your world upside down." He nodded in agreement.

The concept of "conversion" fascinates me. For some it's dramatic. Others it's a slow, gradual process over years. Some spend their lives hoping something dramatic happens—and it never does. In this situation, God dramatically showed up as my friend dropped a barrage of four-letter words heavenward. I don't understand why—few clergy I know would ascribe this as a method of getting closer to God.

"The curses of the ungodly are more pleasing to God's ears," wrote Martin Luther, "than the hallelujahs of the pious." I think Luther understood that God appreciates honesty. God handles truth—the truth of how we feel, what we're thinking and what we're experiencing. If we're in the dumps, God can handle it. No shame. No judgment. Pretending is dishonest—it's actually separating us from God.

In the Bible, these honest outbursts are called laments. Unfortunately, it's a part of the Christian tradition that's often forgotten, replaced with the compulsion that a "strong faith" means uninterrupted bliss and happiness. But that's not real life. When our lives are overcome with chaos, brokenness, suffering, death, and a sudden sense of our vulnerability, we can't just pretend everything is okay.

"O God, find me!" penned the poet Ann Weems after the death of her 21-year-old son. "I am lost in the valley of grief, and I cannot see my way out."[17]

In his time of isolation, Jesus recited a Psalm of lament when he cried: "My God, my God, why have you forsaken me?" Another Psalm records, "How long, O Lord? Will you utterly forget me?" Job spends a few chapters arguing with God about his plight. Real and naked moments. Humans opening their hearts in honesty to God.

Phil Yancey captures this sentiment in his book *Disappointment with God*: "Why the delay? Why does God let evil, and pain so flagrantly exist, even thrive, on this planet?" Yancey unapologetically replies: "God holds back for our sake. Re-creation involves us; we are, at the center of God's plan...our very existence announces to the powers of the universe that restoration is under way."

Our lives are an announcement—restoration is under way! That's hopeful. You and me...part of God's plan. Every honest prayer, every expression of faith, every compassionate response, and every act of justice contributes to God's restorative work. It's not easy. At times we're tempted to quit, withdraw, or utter words we wish we'd never said. Sometimes the pain seems too great to take the next step. But we do. We must. Remember: in those moments of honesty, transparency and vulnerability, God's Spirit finds space to move and transform. Believe in the promise: "For when I am weak, then I am strong." That's where we begin.

REFLECTION

> "The opposite of love is not hate, it's indifference. The opposite of art is not ugliness, it's indifference. The opposite of faith is not heresy, it's indifference. And the opposite of life is not death, it's indifference."[18]
>
> –Holocaust Survivor, Elie Wiesel

> "A community of faith which negates lament soon concludes that the hard issues of justice are improper questions to pose at the throne, because the throne seems to be only a place of praise. I believe it thus follows that if justice questions are improper questions at the throne…they soon appear to be improper questions in public places, in schools, in hospitals, with the government, and eventually even in the courts…the order of the day comes to seem absolute, beyond question, and we are left with only grim obedience and eventually despair."[19]
>
> —Walter Brueggemann

WRITING THE BETTER STORY

1. Do you struggle with being honest with God? Why? Explore the roots of that struggle.

DAY NINE
GIVERS & TAKERS

"Travel is fatal to prejudice, bigotry, and narrow-mindedness, and many of our people need it sorely on these accounts."
– Mark Twain

"My mind was blown," revealed the email. "How could people I didn't know be willing to cover my entire trip?"

I love these serendipitous surprises. It's the best part of my job. A former student, unexpectedly and unannounced, reaches out to me and—with a deep sense of gratitude—reflects positively on the impact UrbanPromise has on their lives.

UrbanPromise is an urban youth ministry that was founded in 1988 in Camden, NJ. Through holistic programs our team hopes to equip inner city children and teens with the skills necessary for academic achievement, life management, spiritual growth and Christian leadership. It's been a joy to watch young people flourish with this opportunity.

Fifteen years have evaporated since a 16-year-old Vernon Mincey traveled to South Africa for a Habitat for Humanity service project with our program. He remembers as if it happened yesterday—precise, clear, and defining.

"I was exposed to a world I didn't know existed," he wrote. "I remember returning to my south Camden neighborhood with a sense of duty... constantly reminding younger kids that they didn't have to become a product of their environment…and challenging them to do better and better."

Vernon now works as a field technician with Maser Consulting, an engineering firm specializing in municipal building projects throughout the Delaware Valley. Every fourth Friday the company collects money for a local charity. This past month, Vernon nominated our organization with a compelling and heartfelt letter to the CEO, sharing the impact UrbanPromise had on his life growing up in Camden.

"With your contributions on this charitable donation Friday," implored Vernon. "I am hoping to help give another inner-city child an opportunity to have their heart and eyes opened." We were selected. $1,500 was collected from the employees at Maser.

This gift—and the story behind it—is a wonderful encouragement to my soul. But beyond the gift, a deeper question is raised—why do some people feel compelled to "give back" to the people (organizations, schools, churches, camps) who impact their lives, whereas others do not?

According to organizational psychologist, Adam Grant, the world is full of what he calls "givers" and "takers." Givers are those living their lives for others—always exploring ways to improve and develop people around them. Givers live beyond self-interest. According to Grant's research, "givers" are the people you want on your teams and in your companies. Their presence leads to greater creativity, greater trust, sharing of knowledge and greater efficiency—even at the cost of their personal advancement.

"Takers," on the other hand, are those advancing their own agenda, striving to one-up their colleagues and protect their self-interest. They can rise quickly in their careers, but on teams they thwart productivity, diminish creativity and create cultures of low trust. Grant argues that many of us fall somewhere between. He calls these in-between folks "matchers"—matching one good deed of altruism against a deed of self-interest. So, here's the question I want to answer: are people born as givers? Or takers? Or matchers?

Kurt Hahn—the German educator of Jewish origin who taught at the prestigious Salem Castle boarding school in the 1930s and refused to sign a loyalty pledge to Hitler—believed "givers" can be nurtured. As Nazism rose to prominence, Hahn fled for his life and landed at the Gordonstown School in Scotland. There he converted to Christianity, renounced his German citizenship, and found his educational imagination illuminated by the parable of the Good Samaritan. Hahn developed the theory and practice of "experiential learning," believing that knowledge, in and of itself, is insufficient for flourishing lives.

"How do we help children become Good Samaritans?" asked Hahn. He believed the parable embodied everything to which a human should aspire—courage, faith, generosity, compassion, attentiveness, tribal transcendence…Yes, Hahn believed in the rigors of good academics. But Nazism reminded him that intelligent people can do horrific things. Young people need to develop virtue, bravery, self-reliance and compassion. For Hahn, the Good Samaritan was an aspirational story with potential to inspire students to transcend the limitations of race, ideology and indifference. A new generation of Good Samaritans, he believed, could protect the world from descending into madness.

Realizing the Good Samaritan is just a story—a parable told by Jesus—its enduring power rests in the truth that we can all find ourselves somewhere in the narrative. Each of us can relate to walking past situations and inviting a response. I can certainly identify with the priest who rushes to his next appointment, missing the opportunity in his path, or the legal scholar who can rationalizes away his ambivalence.

But the Samaritan intrigues us…why does he act so differently? Where does he learn courage, compassion, hospitality? Maybe from a caring mother, a courageous grandparent, an unassuming compassionate neighbor? Perhaps the Samaritan, as a child, received an unexpected generous gift…a trip paid for by an anonymous donor? Like Vernon.

Jesus obviously believed we could nurture Samaritan-like habits. Otherwise, why share the story? If we can't change, can't grow, can't become more giving people, then why tell this parable?

By telling the story, Jesus gives humans a tremendous compliment. Jesus is basically saying: "I believe anyone can become a good Samaritan."

"So much of history is made up of small moves," wrote Seyward Darby, "Hope, too, dwells in increments."[20] Vernon now lives his life as a giver—a young man who wants to pay it forward. That's hopeful. That's incremental. And if enough of us, do it together, we'll change the world.

REFLECTIONS

> "When you saturate a project like this with care and attention, when you establish a real personal relationship, intangibles are a large part of what you provide—and those count for a lot. When there's a high ratio of love to dollars, the payoff per dollar is higher."[21]
> —James Boyce, *Development Economist*

> "I have said that mercy is a journey that goes from the heart to the hands. In the heart, we receive the mercy of Jesus who forgives us everything, because God forgives everything and lifts us up, gives us new life and infects us with his compassion…from that forgiven heart …the journey to the hands begin, namely through the works of mercy."[22]
> —Pope Francis, *The Name of God is Mercy*

WRITING THE BETTER STORY

1. What moments in your life has deepened your sense of compassion?

2. How can you demonstrate compassion this coming week? Is there a specific situation?

DAY TEN
ORDINARY HEROES

"Greater love has no person than this, that they lay down their life for their friends."
–John 15:13

"People's reaction to toilet paper is an interesting case study," shared the woman facilitating our Zoom meeting. "Why is it that some people are hoarding it, whereas others want to make sure their friends and neighbors have enough—and are willing to share their last roll?"

Up until now I hadn't really pondered the psychology of toilet paper accumulation and the statement it makes about our character. It's certainly a fascinating case study and raises questions about human nature—especially in times of crisis. In moments like these, why are some willing to share the shirt off their back, while others are compelled to stockpile their garages? Let's try to answer it.

In the wake of World War II, Samuel Oliner extensively researched why ordinary people act in extraordinary ways in times of crisis. His early research focused on people who had risked their lives to hide and protect Jewish people during the Holocaust. Oliner observed basically three kinds of people: collaborators with the Nazis, those who looked the other way, and those who courageously acted against them. The common thread uniting those who acted, concluded Oliner: *high levels of empathy*. Rescuers felt the pain of others.

Later research moved Oliner to interview recipients of the Carnegie Hero Fund Commission—people who are recognized for civilian heroism. The definition of the award: "A civilian who knowingly risks his or her own life to an extraordinarily degree while saving or attempting to save the life of another person." Engraved on every Carnegie medal is the biblical injunction from John 15:13: "Greater love has no person than this, that they lay down their life for their friends."

Again, Oliner asked the question: why do these ordinary people—who run into burning buildings to save children, wade into a raging river to save the drowning—intervene when someone is being attacked, or stop by the side of the road to help? What do they have in common?

In 78 percent of the interviews, award recipients mentioned the importance of adult guidance in the formation of moral beliefs. Oliner called it "normocentric" behavior—these "ordinary heroes" learned the importance of caring and social responsibility from older adults and communities that affirmed moral-spiritual values and the forming of close, caring attachments to other people. In short, this kind of selfless heroism didn't just appear in a vacuum. It wasn't a magic rabbit that popped out of a hat. Selfless heroism found expression in times of crisis because value systems have been developed through role modeling, teaching, and the creation of empathic relationships.

Times like this cry out for ordinary heroes. I find it refreshing to see our society moving away from celebrity worship and start to rethink its idea of heroic behavior. Each day, I hear new stories about essential workers—bus drivers, grocery store clerks, health care workers, public servants, cleaners, ambulance attendees, delivery people—who are showing up so we can eat, get to work, enjoy sanitized environments, have safe streets, and have peace that our aging parents are receiving quality care. Ordinary heroes.

Sure, there are those who will still hoard toilet paper…because it's their "right" as a consumer in a free society to buy as much and whatever they please. But my hope and prayer is that those who are currently surrendering personal rights—for their neighbor and the collective good—will find a permanent place in our moral imaginations and hearts, inspiring each of us to new levels of love and service.

REFLECTIONS

"I don't believe one can die from lack of wonder, but I am certain that a deficit of it will ensure that one has never really lived. If that's true, then few of us, including myself, are really truly alive in this anxious age, for anxiety is the great enemy of wonder. Anxiety implores us to retreat; wonder to expand. Ignorance festers in small minds, wonder spreads out from the open one; fear demands that we build walls, wonder that we tear them down."[23]

–Ed Simon

"People are unreasonable, illogical, and self-centered. Love them anyway. If you do good, people will accuse you of selfish, ulterior motives. Do good anyway."[24]

–Anyway Poem, Kent M. Keith

WRITING THE BETTER STORY

1. If anxiety is the great enemy of wonder, and if we need more wonder to really live, how can you cultivate a deeper sense of wonder today?

2. In what ways is anxiety controlling your life? Name those things your anxious about—whether it's a lack of toilet paper, or your lack of job security?

3. Compliment an ordinary hero this week—write about the experience.

DAY ELEVEN
LAST WORDS

"Wake Up."
–Matthew 26:46

A good friend of mine is having trouble sleeping. In the middle of the night, he wakes up thinking about all that is wrong in the world. Even in the best of circumstances he's hardwired to worry—which makes him brilliant as an estate attorney. But being alone in his active brain, in the middle of the night, produces abnormal levels of anxiety.

"Instead of worrying," he shared with me this Sunday morning. "I decided to use the time to write a letter to my children."

"I know I'm sounding a little morbid," he confessed. "I don't think I'll die from the Coronavirus, but I decided to write down everything I've wanted to share with them. You can't necessarily predict the circumstances around your death."

And so, he wrote a beautiful, thoughtful, father-endearing two-page email to his four adult children. He encouraged them, confessed some of his failures as a father, shared his favorite memory with each child growing up, expressed his reason for believing in God and gave them some fatherly advice about living in a world that seems to be unraveling. At 3 a.m., he pressed the send button.

"You need to do it," he challenged me. "I was surprised by the responses of my kids—and their spouses. It's been really encouraging and enlightening."

My friend got me thinking about the importance of last words…and how I can better use this unusual moment to share what I've never had time to share.

Years ago, I heard a memorable interview on NPR with an aging Holocaust survivor. I forget many of the details, but my memory has never released her main point. As a pre-teen girl, she recalled being herded onto a train with other Jewish children. "I was with my younger brother," she remembered. "He lost one of his shoes in the scuffle. I scolded him."

A few minutes later, brother and sister were separated and sent to different concentration camps, never seeing one another again. "It's the biggest regret of my life. My last words to my little brother…I reprimanded him over something as inconsequential as a lost shoe." She concluded, "I've tried to live the remainder of my life carefully choosing the words I speak to people—just in case they are my last." That's a life lesson.

Do you remember the last words Jesus shared with his disciples in the Garden of Gethsemane? "Wake Up." He repeated them twice because his disciples slept through the moment. I'll concede it was a difficult and confusing moment. I would have done the same. But they missed what was happening. In the words of Jean-Pierre de Caussade, they failed to appreciate "…the sacrament of the moment." Blaise Pascal echoes those sentiments when he calls the disciples performance the "Gethsemane Sleep."

I've got some homework to do this week. I need to stay awake to the moment, reflect thoughtfully on words I need to share and write a few letters. When completed, I hope to have the courage to press…SEND.

REFLECTIONS

> "At the personal level, the key to successful living is continuous personal change. Personal change is the way to avoid slow death. When we are continually growing, we have an internal sense of meaning and impact. We are full of energy and radiate a successful demeanor. To have such feelings in a continually changing environment, we must continually realign ourselves with our environment. This requires that we do an unnatural thing—that we exercise the discipline to take an unusually different perspective."[25]
> –Robert Quinn
>
> "Ask yourself: Are you spending your time on the right things? Develop a good filing system. Rethink the telephone. Delegate. Take a time out. Time is all you have. And you may find one day that you have less than you think."[26]
> –Randy Pausch, *The Last Lecture*

WRITING THE BETTER STORY

1. Are there any last words you need to share with someone? A letter to write? An email to send? A phone call to make?

2. What are some ways you'd like to continue to grow—in an effort to avoid slow death? Write them down.

DAY TWELVE
SOW WHAT?

"Whoever sows sparingly will also reap sparingly, and whoever sows generously will reap generously."
–2 Corinthians 9:6

"I just remember being scooped onto a white bus, warm pancakes and love," posted the young woman on Facebook, "I have no doubt we stressed you guys out. Personally, I appreciated all the effort."

Twenty-five years have passed since this 7-year-old girl first walked through the doors of our program in Camden, and what does she remember? An old white bus...Warm pancakes...and...love. Pretty simple. Isn't it fascinating what kids remember—a poignant reminder of what really matters.

A while ago a former intern formed a Facebook group called, "Old Promises" for former missionaries and students. A few photographs were initially posted between the four alumni. Within a few days, close to 300 people were posting and commenting—the contributions grew daily. Former kids and interns were sharing favorite memories, favorite camp songs, current occupations, stories of faith and...re-connecting. During this season of social distancing and uncertainty, there seems to be a growing hunger to connect, especially to those with whom we've shared experiences and history. As I read the comments being posted, I was amazed at the important role this ministry has played in the development of so many lives.

I personally remember the first time that little wisp of a girl was scooped onto our old white school bus. It was Sunday morning. She was picked up with her older sister Yolanda for Sunday school at Rosedale Baptist Church on 27th and Westfield Ave. Her name was Summer Tatum.

Sunday mornings always began with a pancake breakfast for kids like Summer. Volunteers griddled up plates of hot cakes. If it was a good week for donations, a little bacon might end up on a plate—sausages if we hit the lottery. A glass of powdered Tang was always available to wash the syrup down. The quality of the food was certainly questionable, but the weekly ritual of eating a warm meal was never forgotten.

"I'm now serving in the U.S. Army, stationed in Washington, D.C.," continued Summer on her Facebook post. "I'm a CBRNE soldier, so I ensure soldiers are trained and prepared for any type of chemical, biological or nuclear attack."

What? That little girl, who liked to gobble up pancakes, is now protecting our country against chemical, biological and nuclear attacks—how does that happen? I believe it happens when caring adults do the hard work of faithfully showing up and generously planting seeds of love, attention, and faith into the hearts and minds of hurting kids.

"UrbanPromise definitely provided a safe, loving space where I was introduced to Christ," concluded Summer. "That foundation is something that I personally feel most children miss out on today."

When I think of the trajectory of Summer's life and who she has become, I'm reminded of a very simple truth shared to the church of Corinth by the Apostle Paul. St. Paul reminds ordinary people that we can choose to live our lives in a variety of ways. There's no judgment in the verse—just simple logic and a promise. Paul is offering an opportunity for a bigger, richer more blessed life.

"Sow sparingly, and you'll reap sparingly," he wisely offers. "Sow generously and you'll reap generously."

Day Twelve: Sow What?

This past week I experienced the truth of Paul's teaching in a very real way. It's hard to explain in words, but let me try. For the past three decades, a community of God's people—staff, volunteers, donors, churches, board members, teenage leaders—have sown generously into the lives of Camden's children. Summer's story is an example of this generous sowing. Despite all the hardship and despair in our world, I've witnessed an unusual bounty of transformational stories, donations, and words of affirmation. I truly experienced the gift of faithful people who sow generously. It's a gift our world needs right now. Circumstances might beckon us to retreat and play defense. Let's resist and continue.

REFLECTIONS

> "It occurred to me that there were two sets of virtues, the resume virtues and the eulogy virtues. The resume virtues are the skills you bring to the marketplace. The eulogy virtues are the ones that are talked about at your funeral—whether you were kind, brave, honest or faithful."[27]
>
> –David Brooks

> "Part of what we have at HomeBoy is this irresistible culture of tenderness, you know, where people kind of hold each other. It's a place of containment, a place where people can regulate. And they all come with, you know, kind of chronic, toxic stress that's attached to them like a big, old heavy backpack. And if they can find relief then they no longer have to actually operate out of survivor brain, and then they can find our place as something of a sanctuary…"[28]
>
> –Father Greg Boyle, HomeBoy Industries

WRITING THE BETTER STORY

1. When people talk about you at your funeral, what kind of virtues do you hope they will share? Will you be talked about as someone who "sowed generously" or "sparingly"?

2. How can you "sow" more generously today? Be specific.

DAY THIRTEEN
ZIP CODE BURDEN

"God spares us from nothing, while unexplainably sustaining us in all things."
–James Finley, *Mystical Sobriety*

"One of our employees tested positive," shared one of our staff, "I'm trying to track down everyone who had contact this past week."

It was the call I didn't want to receive. Despite the rising numbers of COVID-19-related cases identified in Camden, I had hoped the UrbanPromise community would dodge the proverbial virus bullet. Coronavirus was now personal. An hour later came the second call.

"It looks like 30 volunteers and staff had direct or indirect contact with the individual through the school and Food Co-op," continued my colleague, "We'll need to notify everyone and encourage those showing symptoms to get tested." Our team picked up their phones and began to make calls. It was mindboggling how quickly this virus could spread.

Our ministry continued to show up for the people of our city during the pandemic. Yes, we practiced social distancing, wore masks, and washed hands—but we also tried to keep families fed, children learning and providing the psychological and emotional support needed. Despite the risks, we didn't abandon our post.

Camden made the headlines this past week. Coronavirus cases surged by 2,925% in less than 3 weeks. Reported cases are growing by 19.4%

per day. Why? Why do under-resourced communities, like Camden, seem to always get hit hard? Multiple reasons: Overcrowded housing, multi-generational families living together, hourly workers who continue to provide essential services—in hospitals, nursing homes, grocery stores, fast food restaurants… These are workers who often rely on public transportation. Add a surging homeless population, undocumented families, and workers without health insurance, and the environment becomes a ripe for transmission. Zip codes can tell the story.

There's an old Haitian proverb that claims, "We see from where we stand." Our perspective is shaped by our real estate. And that's okay—to a degree. But God is always nudging us to broaden our vision, our hearts, and our understanding. God's curriculum is about growth, especially when it involves growing in awareness of how others live and suffer.

That's why we need a book like the Bible. It gets under our skin and makes us a little uncomfortable. It's an outside voice, independent of our circumstances and bias', directing us to places and truths we'd rather avoid. I think it was Martin Luther who said the Bible brings "comfort to the afflicted and affliction to the comfortable." A little affliction can be a good thing if it helps us grow.

And so the ancient prophet Micah writes: "God has shown you, O Mortal, what is good and what is required of thee: Do Justice. Love Mercy. Walk humbly with God." (Micah 6:8)

Unfortunately, every generation needs to be reminded of these words. Despite the advances of science, technology and medicine, there always seems to be an imbalance in the world. Mercy is not always in abundance. Some folks get left behind. Some folks are burdened with more than their fair share—especially children.

And so, we need to be reminded that the great responsibility of being human is the privilege to use our gifts and talents to help ease the burden others must carry—and perhaps challenge and question those systems that add to the daily burden. That's what God's people do.

Day Thirteen: Zip Code Burden

The good news is that our infected staff worker is recovering after a harrowing ordeal, and nobody else has tested positive on the UP staff. The bad news is that numbers of COVID-19 cases continue to rise in Camden and we need to do everything we can to address the issue.

This week, let's be intentional about growing our perspective by walking in another's shoes. When we see the scales tipping disproportionately in one direction, let's be doers of justice. I'm sure it'll look different for each of us. "Bear one another's burdens," reminds the Apostle Paul, "and so fulfill the law of Christ" (Galatians 6:2). That's a pretty good place to start.

REFLECTION

> "Love is not doing things for other people; it is revealing to people their beauty, the light shining in them."
> –Jean Vanier
>
> "Dear Child of God, before we can become God's partners, we must know what God wants for us. 'I have a dream,' God says, 'Please help Me to realize it. It is a dream of a world whose ugliness and squalor and poverty, its war and hostility, its greed and harsh competitiveness, its alienation and disharmony are changed into their glorious counterparts, where there will be more laughter, joy, and peace, where there will be justice and goodness and compassion and love and caring and sharing."[29]
> –Bishop Tutu

WRITING THE BETTER STORY

1. How can you intentionally connect more deeply with those who live on the outskirts—and how might this impact your understanding of those who live in the shadows of society?

2. Write of an event in your life where the dividing line between service provider/service recipient was erased? How can that become part of your story?

DAY FOURTEEN
SECOND MILE VACANCY

"The experience of aliveness must never degenerate into a narcissistic celebration of self—for if it does, it dies."
–Parker Palmer

Allow me to try and make a connection between first century Palestine and a contemporary situation. I'm not a biblical scholar, so I'll attempt this as a novice—who knowingly leaves his area of expertise—and ventures to opine on a subject I have no business to do so.

In Jesus' day, Rome occupied Israel—meaning her people were subject to the imperial laws of the Roman emperor. Now, nobody likes to be bossed around by a foreign power, and that was certainly true for the people of Israel. Consequently, flashes of rebellion and resistance would pop up from the locals, which were quickly squelched by Roman soldiers who patrolled the neighborhoods.

There was one government policy that was particularly egregious: if a Roman soldier asked a local to carry his shield, sword, helmet, or Samsonite suitcase—they were required to carry it a mile. Just a mile. After completing the mile, and not a step before, the local could legally lay down the heavy armor and walk away. Follow the rules. No problems.

Now, the locals resented this policy. It violated their freedom and festered anger—a constant reminder that they were guests in their own home. Think about it: you're walking home after a long, tiring day of work. You're a block away from sitting down with your family, having a cool drink and enjoying a quiet evening together. A soldier eyes you: "Hey," he demands, "Carry my stuff."

A surge of indignation pulsates through your veins. You feel diminished as a human being. You want to protest in some way. Run? You quickly remember the fate of your neighbor who tried a few months ago. Cuss him out? That never ends well. File a complaint at the local police station? Not a winning strategy. Then…the words of an itinerate teacher you heard last week flash through your mind.

"If anyone forces you to go one mile, go with them two miles."

On a practical level these words don't make sense. The notion of surrendering a second mile, *voluntarily*, no less, seems so outlandishly generous and unnecessary. On the surface it appears as weakness—you're condoning an unjust law and an oppressive regime by offering more than what the law requires. Surely that's no protest. But that itinerant preacher named Jesus still has your imagination. You give it a try.

The journey with the soldier begins. As you hit the one-mile mark you continue to walk onward. At first the soldier says nothing. "You can stop now," he eventually demands. "You've done what's required!" You smile. *"I'm giving you a second mile today,"* you offer with a wink. "It's on the house." The soldier is perplexed. In all his years of inflicting this pain on hard working people, he's never witnessed such a moment. He feels unsettled. His control is lost because of this voluntary act of generosity. The man with the weapons and law on his side has actually lost his power. A new kind of power is being released—a paradoxical power rooted in love and grace. I can only imagine the conversation between the soldier and the local as they walk the extra mile together. God works during the second mile.

That story brings me to the current situation. Yesterday, walking through a local town, I noticed some people wearing protective masks and others not. We all shared this beautiful public space together, leisurely enjoying the outdoors. If I surveyed the "masked" people and the "unmasked" people, I might get very different responses. One side suggests that wearing a mask protects them and others from the spread of the Coronavirus—their proud civic duty as a member of a larger society. The other group argues that there is no law mandating the mask, it's their God-given right to exercise their freedom, and there's no conclusive medical proof that masks prevent the spread of these destructive germs. And so, we end up with two camps of people, equally convinced that their position is the right one, ready to hold their ground as they look upon one another with possible suspicion.

But Christians are unusual people—we're people of the second mile. And as the saying goes: "It's never crowded on the second mile." The second mile lifestyle is the third alternative to those who only see the world as "us" and "them." Perhaps that's why there's so little traffic—it's hard to let go of our labels and move to a place where our power is exercised with grace and extravagant generosity.

What's remarkable about Jesus is he's always pointing us to a bigger vision of ourselves—a vision that calls us to live beyond the letter of the law, beyond the bare requirements of civility, beyond pettiness and beyond our personal entitlements. It's actually his ultimate compliment: Jesus believes we are capable of extraordinary behavior. "Greater love has no one than this" he affirms, "than to lay down our lives for a friend." The capability to transcend our self-interest lives in each of us.

"Love takes off the masks we fear we cannot live without," wrote James Baldwin, "and know we cannot live within." As we move forward in the coming years to rebuild our communities, I pray that we'll move beyond the false masks and labels that divide us. I pray that we'll find joy in the privilege of surrendering our individual rights so others can flourish. I pray that we will take this opportunity to reimagine a new kind of world—the world of the second mile.

REFLECTIONS

"Let us not fall into indifference but become instruments of God's mercy. All of us can be instruments of God's mercy, and this will do more good to us than to others because mercy passes through a gesture, a word, a visit, and this mercy is an act of restoring the joy and dignity which has been lost."[30]

–Pope Francis, *The Name of God is Mercy*

WRITING THE BETTER STORY

1. Write about the moment you stepped out onto the "second mile"–what did you learn?

2. How might you surrender your "rights" this week for the sake of others?

DAY FIFTEEN
ACHING VISIONARIES

"If one part suffers, every part suffers with it; if one part is honored, every part rejoices with it."
−1 Corinthians 12:26

Once a month, our team gathers to share, laugh, pray, celebrate accomplishments, and encourage one another. We see ourselves as a community—more than a program, more than a service provider, and more than an educational institution. The vibrancy of our programs flows from our unity as a community.

So, I think the words of the Apostle Paul to the church at Corinth (1 Corinthians 12:26) are particularly relevant to all of us connected to this mystical community, especially this week in light of our country's tragic events:

> "If one part suffers, every part suffers with it; if one part is honored, every part rejoices with it."

Paul eloquently casts a vision of the burden and joy of being part of this sacred community that transcends race, geography, economics and ethnicity. Paul is not describing a country club membership, a college fraternity or a monolithic group of people connected for reasons of self-interest. St. Paul is describing a different kind community—a group of people connected to one another by faith and love in Christ. This is the commitment we make. We voluntarily move into the lives and worlds of those we may not know, having very few things in common, even disagreeing and sharing radically different histories. Our capacity to suffer expands because of our union…as does our capacity for joy.

That's why I want to invite you to one of our team meetings during the height of the racial unrest in America during the summer of 2020. I want you to hear the voices of our community as they process the deaths of George Floyd and Ahmaud Arbery.

"I was watching an innocent children's program on Channel 3 with my 8-year-old son," shared one of my female colleagues, her voice heavy with emotion. "Part way through the program it switched to a "Breaking News Update" and there was George Floyd with an officer's knee on his neck in my living room. My son was visibly shaken. At that moment I knew I had to have 'the talk.'"

Some in our group needed to be schooled on what "the talk" means. So, we listened intently as our colleague described what it's like to be an African American mother, having to discuss the realities of race in America with a curious and rambunctious boy. "It's not a conversation I want to have," she lamented. "I see stuff like this, and I'm terrified for my child." We listened and tried to honor her fear and pain.

"As a white male," shared another colleague, "the only talk I'll have with my kids is a conversation about safe sex. I'll be candid, I never really think about the safety of my kids walking through our neighborhood. I'm sorry you must have these conversations."

"You know," added another, his face buried deep in his hands. "I was a student at UCLA during the Watts riots…I just can't believe we are still dealing with these forms of racism 30 years later. It's like we're moving backwards."

One of the more senior women in the group jumped into the conversation. "My father was chased 3 times by the KKK," she recounted from her days growing up in the south. "I've raised 3 sons. I know what it's like to worry."

Day Fifteen: Aching Visionaries

"The saddest part of having our schools closed," concluded another, "Is that we can't have these kinds of discussions to help our students process this moment and strategize solutions." As a group, we continued to listen, trying our best to honor the varied experiences of our group.

Over the past three decades, our ministry has tried to build an intentionally diverse community. We've tried to create something reflecting and celebrating the breadth and width of God's human creation. It has not always been easy, and it often feels quite fragile. But I believe diverse communities create opportunities for us to grow bigger as people—our lives expand because we welcome the experiences and perspectives of others. And in this moment, when parts of our community hurt, we have all been given the privilege of "…bearing one another's burdens" and so fulfilling "the law of Christ." It's critical we stay together and not fragment.

As a Christian leader, the husband of an African American woman of 37 years and 3 adult children trying to make sense of their racial identity in our world, I keep returning to Jesus as my source of hope and inspiration. As this man—fully human—suffered a painful, inhumane, and unjust death on a cross he continued to extend forgiveness to those who suffered beside him. Even in his pain, Jesus blessed others. And even until his last breath, Jesus extended an invitation to become part of a realm called the kingdom of God—a place of justice, a place of peace, a place of love and a place of forgiveness. We are challenged to do likewise.

"Thy Kingdom come, Thy will be done, on earth as it is in heaven," prays our Lord. In the words of theologian Nicholas Waltersdorf, God's people are called to be "aching visionaries." We long for God's realm on earth and our hearts ache when we experience situations, events and systems that contradict this vision. Racism, violence and poverty are not part of God's vision. They have no place and must be resisted on all levels.

My prayer is that each of us will continue to ache for the things that break the heart of God—and that our aching will lead to sustained, enduring action. My prayer is that we will not grow weary of doing the hard, tedious, intentional and courageous work of making our neighborhoods more just, more safe and more hospitable to all her people.

REFLECTION

> "I remember resigning from my law firm, telling my senior partner that I was going to the Philippines to rescue children from brothels. He just started laughing. He wasn't trying to be rude; it was just so ridiculous. And I had no argument for him. I was just looking at God and saying, "I know that you hate violence. I know that you want it to stop. I know that your plan is to build your kingdom here, your plan is for redemption, is through your people, your church, and so I'm going to go." I thought I might die, or more likely, I'll just fail a slow, miserable death and come home, ashamed and embarrassed. But God just showed up over and over again…now we have 100 staff in the Philippines and the country has been transformed."[31]
>
> —Sean Litton, IJM President

WRITING THE BETTER STORY

1. Write down some of the injustices you see in the world that break your heart—why do they break your heart?

2. How will you protest the wrongs you see in the world? How will you use the gifts God has given you to further the reign of God?

DAY SIXTEEN
SHATTERED DREAMS

"Let us keep moving with the faith that what we are doing is right, and with the even greater faith that God is with us in the struggle."
–Martin Luther King, Jr.

Sixty years ago, on April 5th, 1959, Rev. Martin Luther King Jr—at the age of 30—delivered a sermon called "Shattered Dreams" to his congregation at Dexter Avenue Baptist Church in Montgomery, Alabama. I marvel at its depth and enduring significance.

That particular Sunday morning, King preached from an obscure verse of scripture in the book of Romans: "When I take my journey into Spain, I will come unto you." (15:14).

King reminded his congregation that the Apostle Paul dreamed of traveling to Spain to share the Gospel. As he would make that arduous trip from the Middle East across the Mediterranean, Paul promised to stop in Rome to visit a small and vital community of Christian believers—a community of people he deeply loved. This was Paul's dream—his destiny. Yet the dream was never fulfilled. Paul never made it to Spain and instead arrived in Rome as a fugitive to be confined to a small jail cell.

"Very few, if any, of us are able to see all our hopes fulfilled," emphasized the young preacher. "Paul's life was the tragic story of a shattered dream and blasted hope."[32]

At this point in the sermon, King brilliantly pivots and asks his congregation the million-dollar question: "What does one do under such circumstances?" Or to put it more directly: *how do we deal with our shattered dreams?*

According to King, people tend to deal with disappointment, shattered dreams and unfulfilled hopes in three ways: The first is bitterness and resentment. It's a "coldness of heart" and the development of "hatred for life itself." King adds that we take our anger and bitterness out on those closest to us—children, spouses and our neighbor. These kinds of people "love nobody and they demand no love."

The second way people deal with their shattered dreams is withdrawal. They detach themselves from what is going on around them. At the cost of self-induced psychological and physiological damage caused by repression reminded King, "they attempt to escape the disappointments of life by lifting their minds to the transcendent realm of cold indifference."

The third way is fatalism. King believed this was particularly dangerous for religious folk. People resolve that everything is foreordained and inescapable. They believe that people have no freedom: "Everything is God's will, however evil it happens to be." King admits that in order to preserve human freedom, God does permit evil. But there is a difference between permitting something and ordaining something. It's a dangerous mindset, according to King, to just throw up one's hands and surrender one's disappointments and call it "the will of God."

So, what is the answer?

Honestly confront your shattered dreams and believe that almost anything that happens to us can be woven into the bigger purposes of God. "On the one hand we must accept the finite disappointment," King concludes. "But in spite of this we must maintain the infinite hope. This is the only way that we will be able to live without the fatigue of bitterness and the drain of resentment."

Day Sixteen: Shattered Dreams

That "infinite hope"—in the face of very real disappointments—led this pastor (without a national stage at the time) to act on a local level by organizing the Montgomery Bus Boycott in a church basement—an event that propelled the civil rights movement forward. King did not resign himself to bitterness; neither did he ignore the injustices in his city, nor did he decide that segregation was simply God's will. For months on end, a handful of his congregants met, prayed, hoped and planned how best to act as God's people in that moment.

Some of you may be dealing with shattered dreams—the loss of a career, the closing of a business you spent years building, a dissolved marriage, a wayward child, a scandal in your church…all real disappointments. All asking for a response.

So, we have choices: bitterness and resentment. Indifference. Fatalism. Or infinite hope in the face of disappointment—a hope that forces us to engage our disappointment and propels us to act in ways that reflect the heart of God.

Fortunately, we have examples of those who went before us. Both St. Paul and Dr. King Jr. refused to resign themselves to bitterness, cold indifference or to a toxic fatalism. They faced their disappointments, dug deeper into their faith, looked for God's deeper purpose and continued to act as followers of Jesus. We must do likewise.

REFLECTION:

"Concerning all acts of initiative (and creation), there is one elementary truth, the ignorance of which kills countless ideas and splendid plans: that the moment one definitely commits oneself, then Providence moves too. All sorts of things occur to help one that would never otherwise have occurred. A whole stream of events issues from the decision, raising in one's favor all manner of unforeseen incidents and meetings and material assistance, which no man (or woman) could have dreamt would have come his way."[33]
—William Hutchinson Murray

"Many studies—of spouses' interactions, people's diaries, workers' moods, customers' ratings—have shown that a negative event or emotion usually has at least three times the impact of a comparable positive one. So to come out ahead, we suggest keeping in mind the Rule of Four: It takes four good things to overcome one bad thing...plan on at least four compliments to make up for one bit of criticism."[34]
—John Tierney & Roy F. Baumeister

WRITING THE BETTER STORY

1. Write about a disappointment or "shattered dream"—how has it impacted you?
2. What's a new dream God is birthing in you? How might you deal with opposition and challenges to that dream?

DAY SEVENTEEN
WHY PROTEST?

"The greatest danger in turbulent times is not the turbulence, but to act with yesterday's logic."
–Peter Drucker

"You've spent the last two Saturdays protesting peacefully in Camden," I asked. "Why are you marching?"

On the other end of the Zoom call was 23-year-old Dominic Bowman. I've known "Dom" since he arrived at summer camp in first grade. He never left. I think he's participated in about every program we ever offered. Even after high school, he kept in touch and keeps giving back. If UrbanPromise had a frequent flier club for hours logged at our ministry, Dom would have Executive Platinum status.

Recently graduating from Rider University with a master's degree in organizational leadership, Dom reached out to me about starting his own non-profit organization. After a grueling battle with breast cancer during his sophomore year, Dom's mother passed away. He wants to honor her legacy through the creation of a foundation. But before discussing the ins and outs of non-profit start-ups, I wanted to hear the heart behind this young protester.

"I really want to change the mindset of our kids," he began. "I want to be a leader in all facets. I want them to see that you don't have to resort to gang violence, don't have to resort to guns, you don't have to be an athlete or a rapper. You can be a normal guy with a degree and make a difference. That's all I ever wanted to do—show people they can make a difference."

"So what's your hope for the protests?" I continued. "What kind of change do you want to see?"

"I do hope we see changes in policing," he emphasized. "A different kind of training and approach. But it needs to go beyond police brutality. I really hope it wakes the world up."

"Wake the world up?" I questioned.

"We just want to live on an equal playing field. We just want to be treated fairly, equally and treated like humans want to be treated. That's the biggest thing for me."

I find Dom's words inspiring and challenging—a young man willing to wake up early on Saturday mornings so he can help "wake up the world." I need to listen.

Dominic joins a lineage of protesters going back to the beginning of our country. I often feel Americans suffer from a kind of historical amnesia—or a selective amnesia. We forget that this history of the United States has been significantly influenced through moments of protest. Wasn't it a bunch of patriots who stood up to the mighty British empire in Boston? Wasn't it our sisters, mothers and grandmothers who camped outside the White House—and were unjustly jailed—so they could be fully humanized and given the dignity to vote? Wasn't it a bunch of millworker children who marched from the Kensington section of Philadelphia to President Theodore Roosevelt's summer home in New York, protesting the exploits of child labor and demanding an 8-hour workday and Saturdays and Sundays to enjoy the fruits of our labors? And wasn't it our brothers and sisters of color who withstood the humiliation of fire hoses, German shepherds, segregated public facilities and tear gas to pass civil rights and voting legislation? When Americans sense an injustice, our democracy gives us space to speak up. Protests remind us of our core values and call us to live up to

Day Seventeen: Why Protest?

the ideals of liberty and justice for all.

Christians also need to understand our faith has roots in protest. Sadly, we don't hear many sermons preached by the prophets; Amos, Micah, Isaiah, and Jeremiah. They seldom make the top ten Sunday morning sermon list. Quite frankly, these ubiquitous voices make us uncomfortable. When Isaiah cries out: "Woe to those who decree iniquitous decrees, and the writers who keep writing oppression…turn aside the needy from justice and rob the poor of their right,"—it metaphorically rains on the Bach Mass in B Minor organ prelude.

Like Dominic, these prophets also spoke out for an equal playing field—because when humans are not treated like humans, it's an affront to our Creator. Prophets remind us, as do protesters.

Historically protests have a specific focus, for a specific moment, addressing a specific issue. They don't neglect or dismiss or diminish the myriad of other issues that need to be addressed. So, at this particular moment in history, we are invited, because of this current convergence of events, to bring our voices and resources to the very real problem of racial justice and demonstrable and repeated expressions of violence towards our brothers and sisters of color.

It was a community of Christians who helped Dominic as a leader, as a Christian and as a young man who wanted to make a difference in the world. As a child he needed a summer camp. People provided. As a middle schooler, he needed a Bible study and a spring break trip. People provided. As a teen he needed a job, college preparation and a chance to grow as a leader. People provided. As a college student, he needed a little help with tuition and books. People provided. A community produced this transformational leader.

Inspiring, challenging and hope-filled.

REFLECTION

"To be fully alive is to act. The capacity to act is the most obvious difference between the quick and the dead. But action is more than movement; it is movement that involves expression, discovery, re-formation of ourselves and our world. I understand action to be any way that we can co-create reality with other beings and with the Spirit…To be fully alive is to contemplate…I understand contemplation to be any way that we can unveil the illusions that masquerade as reality and reveal the reality behind the masks. One of the great threats to full aliveness is the sleight of hand practiced by our egos and our culture to keep us from seeing things as they are."[35]

–Parker Palmer

WRITING THE BETTER STORY

1. Is your action more than movement? How does it involve "expression, discovery, re-formation" of yourself and your world?

2. In what ways do you contemplate so that you can see "things as they are?"

DAY EIGHTEEN
SPURS & BURRS

"Let us consider how to spur one another on towards acts of love and good deeds."
–Hebrews 10:24

There's one moment in my life that may remotely compare to the feelings many people are currently experiencing. It was a moment when time seemed to stand still—my future completely beyond my control. My problem could not be fixed, solved or reorganized. Exhausted from sleepless nights, my capacity to focus on anything else was futile. Prayer…impossible. I only wanted to be transported out of the current mess and placed in the future. But that's not how life works. We must live through those unbearable moments.

Unexpectedly, my wife's water broke 23 weeks into the pregnancy of our second child. Four days later, our little girl was born at 1 lb., 2 oz, with severely underdeveloped lungs and a damaged brain. Neonatologists predicted a 10 percent survival rate. Forecasts got worse with each harrowing day she was on life support. Even if she survived the critical first week, she'd be blind with severe cognitive damage…she would not walk…play…learn…

So, what does a person do when their faith waivers, their life equilibrium is disrupted and the capacity to care for oneself spiritually and emotionally is depleted? It does happen. There is no shame in feeling this way.

That's where I found myself. I didn't know how to dig my way out.

There's a deeply profound verse in the epistle to the Hebrews. It's been my truth. Scholars tell us that this ancient community of believers were persecuted, tired, weary and ready to throw in the towel:

> "Let us consider how to spur one another on," urgently writes the author. "Towards acts of love and good deeds" (Hebrews 10:24-25).

It's pretty clear: our spiritual vitality and healing is connected with others speaking into our lives. Our faith might be personal—it's not private. We need people who consider us and spur us beyond our stagnation and despair.

Social scientists call this phenomenon *emotional contagion*. Our words, actions and attitudes infect the people with whom we contact. Studies reveal that receiving a simple smile or positive greeting increases our happiness by 15 percent. The next person we encounter—their happiness increases by 10 percent…and so on. Our levels of courage, compassion, love and generosity infect others as well. This is how we can spur others on.

Emotional contagion has a dark side as well. "Like secondhand smoke," says Daniel Goleman, "the leakage of emotions can make a bystander an innocent casualty of someone else's toxic state." Negativity, hate and scapegoating are also infectious—they don't spur us towards anything good. I call these folk *burrs*. A burr gets under a horse's saddle and causes severe pain and agitation, often distracting the animal from fulfilling its purpose. You've probably met a burr or two in your life.

Thirty-two years ago, when my life took a dramatic and abrupt turn for the worse, some amazing people "spurred" me and our family on with love, encouragement, prayer and generosity. I'm forever grateful. My challenge today is to be intentional about considering others and spurring those around me towards love and good deeds. I hope you'll do likewise.

Day Eighteen: Spurs & Burrs

REFLECTION

> "To love is to be vulnerable. Love anything, and your heart will be wrung and possibly be broken. If you want to make sure of keeping it intact, you must give your heart to now one...Wrap it carefully round with hobbies and little luxuries, avoid all entanglements, lock it up safe in the casket or coffin of your selfishness..."[36]
>
> –C.S. Lewis

> "Much more important are things like whether a job provides a sense of autonomy to act on your unique expertise. People want to work alongside others whom they respect (and, optimally, enjoy spending time with) and who seem to respect them in return...and finally, workers want to feel that their labors are meaningful...we want to feel that we're making the world better, even if it's as small a matter as helping a shopper find the right product at the grocery store. 'You can be a salesperson, or a toll collector, but if you see your goal as solving people's problems, then each day presents 100 opportunities to improve someone's life, and your satisfaction increases dramatically.'"[37]
>
> –Barry Schwartz

WRITING THE BETTER STORY

1. List some people you can "spur" this week to acts of love and good deeds. Write about how you spur these folk.

2. Are there ways you can integrate this practice of "spurring" into your place of work, your family or your church?

DAY NINETEEN
LOVE WASTEFULLY

"Why this waste?"
–Matthew 26:9

The reporter held the microphone close to the retiring bishop's mouth.

"If you we're to boil it down to a few words," he inquired, "what should define Christian behavior?"

The aged cleric stroked his scrappy beard. After decades of ecclesiastical service—baptisms, funerals, communions, weddings—he was in no rush to answer the impatient young journalist. Silence lingered for a few painful seconds.

"Christians," he finally replied, "Christians…are people who love with waste. We are called to be wasteful lovers."

These words created some dissonance for me as a young seminarian, having never put love and waste in the same sentence. Growing up in a household that frowned on throwing anything away, I developed an early aversion to waste. My lunch bucket was a recycled Oreo bag—with an old mayonnaise jar doubling as a thermos for my powdered milk. I was even expected to bring them home every day from school so they could be used again and again! "Waste not, want not" was a mantra seared into my consciousness. I still feel guildy throwing away a Starbucks cup.

But here was a retiring man of the cloth saying the essence of Christian behavior is to love *wastefully?* Shouldn't love be invested like a good mutual fund? You know, sprinkle it around, minimizing risk, making sure we get the best return on our investment? And what about stewardship? Why would a clergy propose to "waste" anything—especially love?

The Jesus story is really a story about wasteful love. It begins with an unknown woman sharing her most valued possession and ends with a man laying down his life for others. Scholars suggest that the first authentic Christian in scripture is the anonymous woman in Matthew's gospel account, known as The Anointing at Bethany. That woman is the only one who understands what's really going on, generously surrendering her expensive perfume, and preparing Jesus for what's coming next—his death and burial.

"Why this waste?" protest the disciples with righteous indignation as she anoints Jesus. "This perfume could have been sold at a high price and the money given to the poor."

To everyone's surprise, Jesus doesn't agree with his buddies. He doesn't throw the woman under the proverbial bus or dismiss her gesture as foolish sentimentality. Jesus elevates her action, offering a less than subtle rebuke: "She has done a beautiful thing for me…and her story will be told forever."

Once again, his disciples missed the point. They failed to see the heart behind the act. It's easy to do. As the leader of a non-profit who spends much of his life asking for donations, I can identify with the disciples. Sell perfume on eBay. Get the cash. Make a significant donation to your local food bank. That's practical. But I miss the point. I miss the heart.

I meet a lot of amazing Christians during my travels. In general, we do a pretty good job of loving others. But often our love is a practical, appropriate, boundary-abiding, a get-something-in-return kind of love. It's love, yes. But it's often safe and calculated.

Day Nineteen: Love Wastefully

Jesus is different. He's a threat to those in power. Why? Jesus could never quite follow the rules of those who determined who and who should not be loved. This ruffled more than a few ecclesiastical feathers. Jesus loved across lines of race and gender. He loved across geographical and religious barriers of his day. So, he made enemies. It cost him his life.

And this is part of the Christian message of Hope. We can invite this spirit of Christ to enter our sometimes small, crusty, fear-filled, boundary-abiding hearts and liberate us to love—wastefully.

REFLECTION

> "What I regret most in my life are failures of kindness. Those moments when another human being was there, in front of me, suffering, and I responded…Sensibly. Reservedly. Mildly."[38]
>
> –George Saunders, Syracuse University

> "Walk down these crowded streets with a smile on your face. Be thankful you get to walk so close to other humans. It's a privilege. Don't let your fellow humans be alien to you, and as you get older and perhaps a little less open than you are now, don't assume that exclusive always and everywhere means better. It may only mean lonelier. There will always be folks hard selling you the life of the few: the private schools, private planes, private islands, private life. They are trying to convince you that hell is other people. Don't believe it. We are far more frequently each other's shelter and correction, the antidote to solipsism, and so many windows on this world."[39]
>
> –Zadie Smith

WRITING THE BETTER STORY

1. Reflect on the past 24 hours, detail by detail. Ask yourself if there were moments you could have loved more "wastefully."

2. What are your regrets of the past week? Are there themes? What do those themes tell you?

DAY TWENTY
NOT THE ROAD

"It's not the road you travel—it's how you travel the road."
–Soren Kierkegaard

One of the great philosophical minds of the 19th century—Danish philosopher and theologian Soren Kierkegaard—writes a poignant meditation on the biblical parable of the Good Samaritan. You know the story well.

One day three men walked down an ordinary, dusty, middle eastern dirt road. All of them were on the same road. Presumably the same day. Nothing special about the road. Yet one man stopped and responded in a way the displayed the heart of God. That's the man Jesus elevated and called our attention towards.

"It's not the Road you travel," insightfully captured Kierkegaard, "It's how you travel the road."

His point is direct and clear. The actual road is NOT of critical concern. It's inconsequential. What's consequential is *how* the road is traveled. Three men. Same road. Two men are inattentive and blind to the moment. One man traveled with an open heart, turning an ordinary walk into an opportunity to reflect the love and compassion of God. *It's not the road.*

I find Christians often getting caught up in what I call "the other road syndrome"—always looking for another, better, easier, grass-is-greener kind of road. It's our nature. "One day," we lament, "when I get on the right road, the better road, the more secure road…then I'll begin traveling with the attentiveness and goodness of the Samaritan."

It's not the road.

Some of us are on a road we would never choose to travel. Given the choice, we'd exit this road and take the nearest off-ramp. Some of us are separated from our kids, worried about our parents in their retirement homes, concerned about the balance in our 401k, wondering if we'll have a job next month, feeling like we're wasting time… Who would choose this road? It's a difficult road we're on.

But this is *our* road…for the moment. So, let's engage like the Samaritan. Let's travel differently.

The apostle Paul reminds us that the reason Christians travel differently is because of our unique wardrobe. We have been given a different set of clothes. Our travel bags possess a special set of garments:

"As God's chosen people…clothe yourselves with compassion, kindness, humility, gentleness and patience (Colossians 3:12). This is our clothing. God's grace and courage as your transform your difficult roads this week into a display of God's transformative power.

REFLECTION

> "I do not see the road ahead of me. I cannot know myself, and the fact that I think I am following your will does not mean that I am actually doing so. But I believe that the desire to please You does, in fact, please You."[40]
>
> –Thomas Merton

Day Twenty: Not the Road

"When Greg Dyke became Director-General of the BBC in 2000, he went to every major location and assembled the staff. They came expecting a long presentation. He simply sat down with them and asked a question: 'What is the one thing I should do to make things better for you?' Then he listened. He followed this with another question, 'What is the one thing I should do to make things better for our viewers and listeners?' He knew that at that early stage he could learn more from his employees than they could from him. The workers at the BBC had many wonderful ideas that they were keen to share. The fact that the new boss took time to question and then listen earned him enormous respect."[41]

–Paul Sloan

"'What do you want me to do for you?' Jesus asked him. The blind man said, 'Rabbi, I want to see.'"

–Mark 10:51

WRITING THE BETTER STORY

1. How can you engage your "road" with more authenticity, more attentiveness, and more compassion?

2. How can you use questions to connect more deeply with the road on which you find yourself—questions for your colleagues, your children, your students, or your neighbors?

3. Jot down a few questions so you can be ready for that moment "on the road."

DAY TWENTY-ONE
WHAT'S IN YOUR HAND?

"And the Lord asked Moses, 'What is in your hands?'"
–Exodus 4:2

Building wooden boats at UrbanPromise involves a lot of sanding—wood, fiberglass and epoxy. For the kids, it's their least favorite part of the build. It's tedious, time consuming and dusty. Tiny, harmful irritating particles fill the air while they work.

So, every student in the shop must wear a high quality, industrial N95 face mask to protect their lungs—the same kind of masks that were needed by our frontlines healthcare workers during the pandemic.

"We had 160 brand new masks in our storage closest," revealed Tommy Calistero, our BoatWorks Director. "I contacted a friend at Cooper Hospital. They desperately needed masks for their frontline workers."

Wait a minute? A small, grassroots, community-based non-profit—that has literally lived hand to mouth for 36 years—donated to a local hospital with millions of dollars in assets? Yes! Cases of brand-new masks were delivered.

"What is in your hands?" asks the Lord of Moses.

You remember Moses? He was that reluctant leader in Exodus who never felt worthy of the challenge to which God has called him. A flawed man, full of self-doubt and excuses—gladly passing off responsibility to the next guy in line.

Moses looked down at his hands. He saw nothing at first glance. Just some blistered fingers and calloused palms belonging to a fugitive Shepherd. But he looked again. An old worn stick? That can't be of any significance!

"Throw it on the ground," said the Lord. A decision confronted Moses. Was he hallucinating? Should he respond? Walk away? Ignore? Laugh?

Moses obeyed and threw the stick to the ground. To his utter surprise, the stick became a snake. And this stick—now in the hands of a man who opened his heart to the possibilities and direction of God—became an instrument used to liberate a burdened and oppressed people.

A fellow urban minister, Bob Lupton, writes: "And so it has been down through history—God using the ordinary assets of ordinary men and women to accomplish divine purposes." Bob is spot on. It's the boy with the fish and the loaves. The widow with a few coins…

What is in your hands? A stick? A skill you've forgotten? A spiritual gift? A cell phone?

I've challenged our community to ask this very question. For many of us it's been a week of re-inventing, re-tooling, and re-purposing. Two weeks ago we had many assets in our hands—clearly defined job descriptions, physical classrooms, chemistry equipment, childcare, transportation, sold out fundraising events…many of these assets are now gone.

Should our team just pack it in? Give up? Lament about the good old days? I don't believe so. It's not God's way. God is always about doing a new thing.

So, our teachers and staff are discovering new assets in their hands—and are witnessing God using these overlooked, forgotten assets to feed our community, educate our children, and connect with our families in deeply purposeful ways.

How about you? What's in your hand needing to be discovered and released for God's purpose this week?

REFLECTION

> "Yes is how you get your first job, and your next job, and your spouse, and even your kids. Even if it's a bit edgy, a bit out of your comfort zone, saying yes means you will do something new, meet someone new, and make a difference."[42]
> –Eric Schmidt, executive chairman of Google
>
> "Every so often, you meet people who radiate joy—who seem to know why they were put on this earth, who glow with a kind of inner light. Life, for these people, has often followed what we might think of as a two-mountain shape. They get out of school, they start a career, and they begin climbing the mountain they thought they were meant to climb. Their goals on this first mountain are the ones our culture endorses: to be a success, to make your mark, to experience personal happiness. But when they get to the top of that mountain, something happens. They look around and find the view...unsatisfying. They realize: This wasn't my mountain after all. There's another, bigger mountain out there that is actually my mountain. And so they embark on a new journey. On the second mountain, life moves from self-centered to other-centered. They want the things that are truly worth wanting, not the things other people tell them to want. They embrace a life of interdependence, not independence. They surrender to a life of commitment."[43]
> –David Brooks,
> *The Second Mountain: The Quest for a Moral Life.*

WRITING THE BETTER STORY

1. What can you say, yes to this week?
2. What unique gifts, talents or assets has God placed in your hands? Are you using what's in your hands to ascend the mountain you are supposed to be climbing?

DAY TWENTY-TWO
SECRET OF CONTENTMENT

"I know the secret of being content in any and every situation…"
–Philippians 4:12

Author AJ Jacobs described himself as "petty and annoyed." He was forgetful of the 300 things that went right for him every day and focused on the 3 things that went wrong. This self-avowed curmudgeon decided he wanted to become a better person—to learn to be more content and grateful. But how? He decided to take a "gratitude journey."

This gratitude journey began by thanking everyone involved in producing his morning cup of coffee. Everyone! You see, the act of noticing is the first act of gratitude.

So Jacobs intentionally thanked the barista who rang him up at his local shop, then found the guy who roasted the beans…and thanked him, too. He called an artist in Seattle who designed the lid for his cup. *Thank you!* He tracked down truck drivers and warehouse workers, the people who picked the beans in Columbia, and the customs workers who guarded the borders. *Thank you!*

Of course, the workers were bewildered. They'd never been thanked. Jacobs even drove out of New York City to the Catskill Mountains and thanked those who guarded the watershed. 99.9 % of our coffee is water, after all. Every *thank you* on his journey turned into a story. New relationships were formed. A deeper appreciation was developed for each person's role in his coffee supply chain.

By the time Jacob finished his "gratitude tour," 1000 people had been thanked. Crazy to consider: a thousand people involved in creating his morning cup of coffee! In retrospect he found himself embarrassed for complaining about paying $2.57 a cup.

Years before AJ Jacobs ever thought about gratitude, the Apostle Paul was eloquently suggesting that he had discovered a "secret"—a secret possessing the power to transform a life.

"I have learned the secret of being content in EVERY and ANY situation," he wrote.

Some of us might react defensively to Paul's claim. "Wait a minute," we refute. "Paul doesn't know the difficulties in my life. He's an ivory tower theologian who is detached from reality."

Not so. Paul wrote those words from a Roman jail—a rather hideous place. Literally holes in the ground where one's family had to provide food to stay alive.

So from this hellish place, Paul wrote—to ordinary, working class folk with no health care or 401ks—that he had learned an important secret: Contentment. An audacious claim, isn't it? Paul challenged us to consider a truth: contentment is a state of being independent from our possessions and circumstances.

Deep down most of know this to be true. We have met people living in bitter poverty…yet they are full of joy. We've known people who have suffered tremendously, yet still forgive and love. We know people who give the shirt off their back, because their needs are secondary to others. History is sprinkled with people who transcend their circumstances to discover the secret of contentment.

I remember a woman named Doris who attended Logan Memorial Presbyterian Church. She was in her late 70s when we met. Her life

Day Twenty-Two: Secret of Contentment

hadn't been particularly easy. After losing her husband to cancer, Doris went back to work as a psychiatric nurse—while raising 4 teenage girls on her own. Despite her very real challenges, Doris always chose gratitude.

For years Doris sent me a $30 dollar gift every month to help our work with inner city youth in Camden, NJ. One day I opened her envelope and a $15,000 check fell out. "Dear Reverend Main," she wrote. "I was going to purchase a new car but decided to send you the money to build your new high school." I was humbled and elated. Two weeks later I received another letter from Doris. "Dear Reverend Main," she began. "Great news! I went to the doctor last week. He said I can't drive anymore. I didn't need my new car, anyway!" What a great attitude. When Doris was diagnosed with cancer, she would always plan a lunch with a friend or trip to movies…after her treatment. "Why should going to the doctor be drudgery?" she shared with me. "Now I can look forward to those visits!" When her eldest daughter had the sensitive conversation about what she wanted to have happen to her body after she died, Doris said with a smile and a wink, "I always wanted to go to medical school!"

But I'll never forget her memorial service when pastor, Reverend Don Painter gave an inspiring eulogy in her honor. "Doris was the most 'pro-choice' person I ever met," he exhorted. Then he clarified. "Not in the political sense. But she always chose joy and gratitude." I believe Doris had discovered the secret of contentment. It's possible.

Henri Nouwan, the late Catholic theologian, said, "Gratitude never comes without effort. The more we choose gratitude in the ordinary places of our day, the easier it becomes."

Why is the apostle Paul so passionate about people learning the secret of contentment? I really believe that content people are liberated to serve more freely. Content people are others-centered—interested and aware of other people's stories and lives. Show me a truly content person and I'll show you a joyful person. The saints of Christianity reveal to us that joy is never found with the accumulation of stuff or the consolidation of power. The saints of the Christian faith show us that joy and peace can be found in the most difficult of human circumstances. Contentment is an inner state of being.

I know I have work to do in this area of my life. My trivial complaints are an indictment of my supposed spiritual maturity. At times I have the audacity to complain when my candied yams are too sweet and my venti triple shot latte with cinnamon sprinkles is too hot. Oh my! And churches can be even worse. I hear complaints about the wrong font size of the bulletin, or the color of the pastor's tie or the fact that bagels have been served for the past three weeks during coffee hour. Come on, saints! It's time we do some self-reflection and start discovering what it can mean *to be content in every and any situation.*

REFLECTION

> "A nationally representative poll conducted by the Kaiser Family Foundation finds that nearly half of all Americans—45 percent—feel that the coronavirus has negatively affected their mental health...When researchers and clinicians look at who copes well in crisis and even grows through it, it's not those who focus on pursuing happiness to feel better; it's those who cultivate an attitude of tragic optimism...Tragic optimism is the ability to maintain hope and find meaning in life despite its inescapable pain, loss and suffering..."
> –Emily Esfahani Smith

Day Twenty-Two: Secret of Contentment

"What set those resilient students apart was their ability to find the good. Unlike the less resilient students, the resilient reported experiencing more positive emotions, like love and gratitude…that didn't mean they were Pollyannas. They did not deny the tragedy of what happened. In fact, they reported the same levels of sadness and stress as less resilient people…In general, resilient people have intensely negative reactions to trauma. They experience despair and stress, and acknowledge the horror of what's happening. But even in the darkest of places, they see glimmers of life, and this ultimately sustains them. It's not the adversity itself that leads to growth. It's how people respond to it."[44]

–Emily Esfahani Smith

WRITING THE BETTER STORY

1. How can you cultivate a deeper sense of gratitude, contentment and resilience when your story is full of despair and suffering?

2. Are there a few practical things you can do today to look for "glimmers of life" and to find this "tragic optimism"?

DAY TWENTY-THREE
POWER OF PURPOSE

"Most of us go to our graves with our music still inside us."
–Oliver Wendell Holmes

I've been to lots of birthday parties over the years—very few match the one I attended recently. First, it was held on Zoom with people attending from across the country. Second, the "birthday boy" turned 100 years old. After perfunctory introductions and the celebratory "this is your life" online slide show, the man of the hour was given the microphone.

"Thy Kingdom come, thy will be done," reverberated the baritone voice through cyberspace. "On earth as it is in heaven." The long-retired pastor paused, caught his breath, and then delivered a 3 minute homily that would rival any preacher in their prime. "We need to be about the business of building God's kingdom of justice, peace and compassion on this earth," he heralded. "That's our mission. Our purpose."

One Hundred years old…and he still possesses the passion, vision and hope to make the world a better place. I find it remarkable.

I first met Dr. Charles Sayre 30 plus years ago when I arrived in Camden. I was a young whippersnapper learning the ropes of urban ministry, trying to figure out which way was up. I had heard about this legendary pastor at Haddonfield United Methodist Church who believed the division between suburban and urban communities was not God's plan, and that the great commandment was to love our neighbors—and not just the one on the other side of our manicured hedge. He walked the walked…literally to Camden.

Over the decades, Dr. Sayre helped birth dynamic and impactful non-profits. Respond Inc was one—impacting the city through job creation and affordable housing. For years he chaired the Fellowship House board in South Camden, a youth ministry organization that served our city for 50 years. Despite his credentials and academic pedigree, he always served with humility. A unifier of people, always kind, and he believed that our mission was the best thing since sliced bread. You can understand why I liked him.

This week I asked Dr. Sayre the secret to his longevity. With his quick and disarming sense of humor he quipped, "Lack of stress"—and chuckled. Naturally adverse to the spotlight, he's always deflected attention from himself. I conclude that his vitality is deeply connected to a faith that drives his unwavering sense of moral purpose. Whatever age, whatever stage of his career, this man always used his influence and power to move people of different backgrounds towards building a world that mirrors God's heart.

Mark Twain had it right when he remarked: "The two most important days of your life: the day you were born and the day you discovered why." Finding the "why" for our lives is critical. And trust me… clergy alone don't have the corner on the purpose market. Every week I meet people discovering the "why" for their existence: business owners leveraging their influence for the greater good, retirees re-purposing their talents to build stronger non-profits, doctors and dentists volunteering their weekends and vacations to help heal our under-resourced communities…the list goes on. Show me a person who has discovered the why of their existence and I'll show you someone with purpose, passion, and joy.

Jesus preached that humans need more than just "bread" and clothing to have full and robust lives. Yes, food is important—and clothes are essential—but each of us needs a larger life vision to feed the deeper hunger of our soul. "Seek first the Kingdom of God," encourages Jesus.

"And all these things will be added unto you." If our priorities are ordered correctly, the rest will fall into place. It's worked for Dr. Sayre.

Not all of us will live to celebrate our hundredth birthday, but I guarantee a life with deep purpose will take us on a journey we'll never regret.

REFLECTION

> "One of the chief requisites for feeling the true joy in life is purpose. A constant in the lives of people who experience a sense of day-to-day aliveness is the discovery of their purpose. We need at our very core to be somebody."[45]
> –Richard Leider, *The Power of Purpose*
>
> "Every organism in the universe has a design–a purpose that determines its function and role. A critical part of our development is the inside-out search for purpose and meaning. The true lesson in life is to turn ourselves inside out to discover that our purpose already exists within."[46]
> –Richard Leider
>
> "This happens in the midst of affluent societies and in the midst of welfare states! For too long we have been dreaming a dream from which we are now waking up: the dream that if you just improve the socio-economic status of people, everything will be OK, people will become happy. The truth is that as the struggle for survival has subsided, the question has emerged: survival for what? Ever more people today have the means to live, but no meaning to live for."[47]
> –Viktor Frankl, The Unheard Cry for Meaning.

WRITING THE BETTER STORY

1. What gives your life a deep sense of purpose? If you're struggling to identify what gives you purpose, write down a few experiences that really gave you a sense of being alive, a sense of joy and a deep sense of meaning. What do those experiences tell you?

2. What does "Seek first the Kingdom of God" mean to you?

DAY TWENTY-FOUR
SACRED SCARS

> *"The things we fear most in organizations—fluctuations, disturbances, imbalances—are the primary sources of creativity."* [48]
> –Margaret J. Wheatley

"What's the significance of the darker rings?" asked one of the visitors. A small group of us gathered around the massive slice of tree trunk—perched vertically like a large, natural billboard.

Pointing to the expansive number of co-centric rings, the park ranger paused for a minute, then replied, "Those are the years of the forest fires. They leave their scars, but the fires didn't kill the trees."

"Actually," he continued to my surprise, "Sequoias *need* fire to survive. The scars become part of their story."

That whole day at the Sequoias National Park was filled with a strange mix of contradictions. "Needing fire to survive," added one more to the list. Hiking the trails was awe inspiring, filling my soul with a sense of majesty and beauty. But against the backdrop of centuries-old trees towering to the heavens, it was hard not to be confronted with a sense of mortality and insignificance reminiscent of the band Kansas—"all we are is dust in the wind."

At 55 years of age, visiting the Sequoias a few hours northeast of Los Angeles was a bucket list moment. Sure, I had seen pictures, but standing at the base of these behemoth living organisms was an incomprehensible experience. As you probably know, the sequoias are the tallest and oldest trees in the world. In this particular grove the oldest tree was 3,000 years. Many live beyond 2,000 years and reach heights of over 1,500 feet. But how is it that the equoias grow so tall and so old? It's pretty simple: they've learned to adapt and survive high altitudes and extreme conditions.

Oddly, fire is actually a friend of the sequoias. Over millions of years, this rare species has developed an impenetrable bark, rich with tannin acids. Insects and animals can't penetrate it, nor can raging forest fires. So, they survive…and grow.

But sequoias also need fire to reproduce. Fire clears forest floors of competing vegetation, leaving behind ash, creating nutrient-rich soil and creating more sunlight for the seedlings. Fire also heats up the cones of the sequoias—cones that sometimes remain closed for twenty years—causing them to release their seeds, which fall to the welcoming forest floor and take root. Ironically, the great threat to the extinction of the sequoia is forest management. When humans interfere with the natural cycles of nature, the conditions needed for reproduction are compromised. There are a few lessons to learn from the sequoias.

It's no surprise that suffering or situations have the capacity to create conditions that lead to growth, creativity and new opportunities. So much great art, literature, spiritual insight, discovery and extraordinary accomplishments are born during moments of crisis. It's one of the paradoxical mysteries of life.

For people of faith, our lives might be best represented by the sequoias cone—cones that have calcified and remained closed for decades. The heat of a crisis opens us up, creating a sense of vulnerability and awakening our hearts to God's spirit.

"Pure gold put in the fire comes out of it proved pure," writes Peter in his epistle. "Genuine faith put through suffering comes out proved genuine."

Day Twenty-Four: Sacred Scars

Inevitably we will emerge from this life with scars. My hope and prayer is that our scars will make our story and faith more genuine and authentic. A better story.

REFLECTION

> "As dancers we work on 'spotting,' the practice of choosing a spot on the wall that becomes our focal point during a turn. To avoid dizziness, the eyes remain focused on the spot. In each turn, the face whips around at the very last moment to return our stare to the same spot...this focused attention of the eyes enables a ballerina to complete 32 *foute* turns or 16 counts of *chaine* turns across the floor without throwing up or reeling across the stage. A flailing arm or a step off balance is the telltale sign that the focal point has been lost. The body follows the clear or muddled focus of the eyes."
>
> "The demands of life often mimic the whirl of a turn. As we spin through our to-do lists, we can lose sight of our spot that orients our life: our faith. With the psalmist, we lift our eyes to the hills—or to the streets, churches, workplaces, malls, or smartphones—but our arms flail and our steps fail, because the hills are not a reliable source of strength."
>
> "The psalmist knows where to spot help and it's not the hills, not other people, and not even one's self. Our help comes from the Lord. Only God can ground us, clear our vision, and help us spin without reeling...God doesn't stop the spinning, but instead offers a spot to give our turning focus."[49]
>
> –Amy Ziettlow

WRITING THE BETTER STORY

1. How do you keep your focus on your faith when the storm or the fire is raging around you?

2. What are some "scars" you carry with you from past fires? How might those scars be used to bless and heal others?

3. Write about "new life" that has been birthed during the fires of your life.

DAY TWENTY-F
PASSIONATE PATIENCE

"...we know how troubles can develop passionate patience in us, and how that patience in turn forges the tempered steel of virtue, keeping us alert to whatever God will do next..."
–Romans 5:3, The Message

The daughter of a colleague works at a local restaurant in a suburban town outside of Camden, NJ. Some restaurants closed during the outbreak of the Coronavirus; others pivoted to takeout only options. Things got slow at times.

One particular night, for whatever reason, business picked up. The combination of a beautiful spring evening with a local population tired of cooking led to a boom in orders. Skelton staffs of hourly workers were overwhelmed—and delivery requests to local homes delayed.

"My daughter arrived home exhausted," shared my friend. "But she was also distraught by the behavior of some customers. People berated the workers for their slow delivery."

"Wait a minute," I interrupted somewhat shocked, "People were rude to the workers?"

"Yes," she replied. "Waiting 2 hours for their sushi, instead of 30 minutes, was too much of an inconvenience."

Berating restaurant workers preparing California rolls and sashimi for people inconvenienced by three weeks of cooking at home…we need to pause for a minute.

An old friend sent me a quote last week: "Crisis doesn't create character; crisis reveals character." I don't agree entirely, but the point is obvious. Warren Buffet puts it another way, "You don't know who's swimming naked until the tide goes out." The tide is going out, my friends. Stress and trouble reveal character—or lack thereof. This might be an opportunity to open our eyes and see what kind of swimwear we've got on.

What I love about the Bible is it's always challenging the reader to go deeper, to look inward, to find purpose in the moment and to do some soul work. It's the Bible where we bump into characters like the apostle Paul who say audacious things like "…troubles can develop passionate patience." *Really?*

Yes, they can. Troubles can teach us patience—but only if we're courageous enough to stop blaming others; to hold the mirror to our lives and do some internal work. Confronting our selfishness and privilege takes courage. Transferring our fear and anxiety onto an hourly worker, who forgets to place a straw in our takeout bag with our chocolate milkshake, is a cheap and easy substitute for what we're called to do during moments like these.

Love is patient, says Paul famously to the church of Corinth. Adversity can be transformed into a gift—a gift that "…forges the tempered steel of virtue, keeping us alert for whatever God will do next."

REFLECTION

> "We still have the fundamental Christian responsibility to love people, and not treat them like dirt. Lots of things have been cancelled by the coronavirus, but love is not one of them."[50]
>
> –James Martin, Jesuit Priest

Day Twenty-Five: Passionate Patience

> "*I choose patience.* I will overlook the inconveniences of the world. Instead of cursing the one who takes my place, I'll invite him to do so. Rather than complain that the wait is too long, I will thank God for a moment to pray.
>
> *I choose kindness.* I will be kind to the poor, for they are alone. Kind to the rich, for they are afraid. And kind to the unkind, for such is how God has treated me."[51]
>
> –Max Lucado

WRITING THE BETTER STORY

1. Write about a situation where you did not demonstrate patience—why? What can you learn from that moment?

2. What has a recent crisis revealed about your character? Is there an area of your life you can work on that might lead to a better story?

DAY TWENTY-SIX
WHICH PARADE?

"...the whole city was stirred and asked, 'Who is this?'"
—Matthew 21:10

One of the most dramatic and overlooked aspects of the Easter story is the triumphal entry of Jesus into Jerusalem. In the story, Jesus enters the city from the east. Scholars tell us of another procession coming from the west—the port city of Caesarea.

During Passover, the city of Jerusalem swelled from 40,000 to 200,000. For an insecure, Rome-appointed political leader—whose charge was to keep his Jewish subjects "in check"—Pontius Pilate sent a Roman Garrison of soldiers to fortify the troops permanently stationed in the holy city. Civil unrest would jeopardize Pilate's appointment.

This parade from the West was visibly stunning—Pageantry, swords, spears, shiny helmets, protruding chests, emotionless faces. And there was Pilate, sitting proudly on his battle-trained stallion.

The parade from the east was markedly different. Instead of spears, there were palm leaves. Instead of well-groomed soldiers, there were poorly dressed peasants. Instead of order and precision, there was chaos. Instead of military cadence, there were shouts of *hosanna in the highest*. And Jesus, the man leading the procession, rides a humble donkey.

The vivid contrast between the two parades was more than simple pageantry. It was also a contrast of world views, of vision, and of mission.

The parade from the west was guided by imperial power and theology. Rome was more than just a city—it was a belief system. It's message was simple: Might makes right! The first shall be first! Intimidate! Consolidate power. Use the poor to your advantage. To the onlooker, Rome seemed invincible. Secure.

In stark contrast, the Jesus parade was guided by a vision laid out in his earlier teachings—a vision that greatness is found in humility, true life is found in surrender, loving your neighbor, caring for the poor, sharing with others, and learning to be agents of healing, peace and grace.

It's no accident that these two parades arrive to the city at the same time. Nothing is accidental with Jesus. Jesus wants us to make a choice between two conflicting parades. And following the Jesus parade takes faith—especially in times of fear and uncertainty.

This is an extraordinary moment in our history. We enter Holy Week with our world literally turned upside down, our heads spinning in disbelief and our feet looking for a stable place to stand. I'm sure the disciples had similar feelings as they followed their donkey-riding leader to the cross.

The Good News of Palm Sunday is that we know our parade is the real deal—it's the parade that endures and lives generationally in those who follow Jesus. Yes, it gets darker before it gets better; there is pain, betrayal, and moments when the light seems to disappear. Hang on. Keep walking. Keep living the vision. We know how our parade ends. It's the parade that continues to change lives and change our world.

REFLECTION

> "Jesus' teachings are not mere suggestions, but pointed challenges to grow. They state urgently, baldly, and sometimes harshly what the "path to life" really is. They are not ideals, but the ultimate practicality. They are statements of the necessary conditions for the flowering of the deepest human capacities, the growth of the *imago Dei*."

Day Twenty-Six: Which Parade?

> "Part of the process of salvation, real soul healing and transformation, is in wrestling prayerfully with the rough places in our souls that resist Jesus' saving invitations."
>
> "Being an apprentice means starting, honestly and humbly, where we are rather than where we should be. We are, in fact, unskilled. The good Master will present us with tasks that are just beyond our reach, tasks that build on our strengths and challenge our weaknesses, and he will stand by us in our clumsiness as we learn."[52]
>
> –Robert C. Morris

WRITING THE BETTER STORY

1. Make a list of four or five of the most important challenges of Jesus—start with the ones you are most familiar with.

2. What would identifiable behaviors look like (both actions & attitudes) that would embody each of these teachings?

3. List some identifiable instances of inability or unwillingness to embody this teaching.

4. Note which of these specific teachings needs more attention in your life. Don't bother with guilt. Guilt may lead to outward conformity, but it does not spur inner-change. Just admit, "I'm not very good at that."

5. Choose one behavior that you might intentionally practice over these next few weeks.

DAY TWENTY-SEVEN
THE FUTILITY OF HATE

"To consider persons and events and situations only in the light of their effect upon myself is to live on the doorstep of hell."
–Thomas Merton

The automatic glass doors of the convalescent home flew open. A delightful blast of cool air—which those who reside in the northeast during August fully appreciate—sent a welcome shiver through my body. Hands moist with perspiration, I feebly gripped the slippery pen and signed my name at the front desk.

Down the hallway in room 106 I would find my 93-year-old friend Mable Smith.

Three weeks prior, Mable had suffered a mild stroke on her way to church. Now recovering, she would be sent home soon when her sense of balance was regained and her vitals stable.

I peeked into the room. The bed was empty. I thought the worst.

"She's in the dining hall," called the orderly across the hallway, with military-like authority. "Keep walking until the end, make a left and you'll see the entrance."

Now Mable was a true character. Feisty. Opinionated. A lifelong Presbyterian. A little eccentric. She spent her career as a Navy secretary and shared with me, on an earlier visit, her harrowing firsthand account of being in Pearl Harbor during the bombing. "Lucky to be alive," she quipped, describing the pandemonium of that 1941 Sunday morning.

"Hi Mable," I gushed, entering the room and giving her a hug as lowered myself into an empty chair next to her. "Who's your friend?"

Across the table sat an aged woman, slowly spooning Tapioca pudding into her mouth with a high level of intentionality. She hardly noticed my entrance.

"This is Chi..yo..ko," mouthed Mable slowly and phonetically, making sure I understood. "She was born in Japan. Survived the bombing of Nagasaki."

I stretched my hand across the table. The woman abruptly and respectfully stopped her methodical motion, placed her spoon on the tray, clutched my fingers and smiled. "Chiyoko," she muttered softly. "Hello."

"We figured we wouldn't be friends if we met in 1942," said Mable. "We were supposed to hate each other back then. Look at us now!"

For the next few minutes, I listened to the story. Somehow Chiyoko survived the blast as a teenager, navigating the horrific aftermath and scraped together a few piecemeal jobs to put food in her stomach. Eventually she met a U.S. serviceman stationed at a base in Japan, learned English, married him and moved to the United States. A widow for over a decade, with no children and outliving her friends, she was essentially alone in the world—except for her new friend Mable.

For whatever reason, I've never forgotten that meal (certainly not the food). Perhaps this week, after reading articles recalling the 75th anniversary of the dropping of the Atomic bomb on Hiroshima and Nagasaki, it triggered my memory. So, without wading into the history and politics as to why those bombs were dropped, I think there's a lesson to learn from a couple of elderly widows who survived a very dark period of our world's history.

Day Twenty-Seven: The Futility of Hate

Maybe the lesson is how the prevailing forces of our historical moment seek to define us as people: influencing our relationships, shaping our values, and dictating our behaviors. Perspectives and attitudes toward people—people we don't even personally know—are consciously and unconsciously shaped by those with the loudest and most convincing voices. As social animals, we even mimic other's behaviors in our quest for identity and belonging.

Then 75 years pass... The cultural, social and geo-political winds change. New enemies are found and created. New wars need to be fought. New people groups need to be feared. But in the end, the lie of our suspicion and fear is exposed by the serendipitous encounter of two convalescing women eating puréed spinach and Gorton's fish sticks together—in (of all places) Cinnaminson, New Jersey. The futility of hate is unveiled by life's brevity and our deepest need for intimacy.

These things we know to be true: Our loved ones will pass on, our workplace colleagues disperse, our children will go their different ways and our political parties voted in and out of office. And, if we are the last one standing, we'll desire only a few elemental things: companionship and love. Ironically—as in the lives of Mable and Chiyoko—both may appear in the form of those we were once told to hate and fear.

James Baldwin wrote, "Hatred, which could destroy so much, never failed to destroy the man who hated."

Jesus put it another way: Love your enemies. Pray for those who persecute you. Turn the other cheek. Why? I always believed Jesus made these outrageous commands because it might lead to more peace, fewer wars and better relations with the neighbor who lets his dog do his business on my lawn. And that can certainly be true.

I bet that Jesus was a few steps ahead of what Baldwin and others would later learn from their firsthand experience, witnessing the corrosive effects of hate—not only on its recipients, but on its givers as well. Perhaps Jesus' commands are really a love letter to you and me from someone who wants to see us flourish and live into the fullness of what we were created to be. The commands are not simply given to win over our enemies. They're actually for our benefit, regardless of the outcome. Creating identities around hate and suspicion produces little people. And Jesus is always about *bigger* people. Bigger hearts, bigger lives, bigger visions.

So why wait until the day we're eating tapioca pudding and fish sticks to expand the companions around our dinner table? Let's rise above the noise of today and tune into the frequency of God's heart. Life's really too short to waste time.

REFLECTION

> "The greatest compliment Jesus ever gave a human being was to love their enemy. Why? Because Jesus believed that humans had the ability to transcend their tribal, barbaric, animal nature and do something truly remarkable."[53]
>
> —Michael Doyle

> "But the plain truth is this: love is not a matter of getting what you want. Quite the contrary. The insistence on always having what you want, on always being satisfied, on always being fulfilled, makes love impossible. To love you have to climb out of the cradle, where everything is 'getting,' and grow up to the maturity of giving, without concern for getting anything special in return. Love is not a deal; it is a sacrifice. It is not marketing; it is a form of worship."[54]
>
> —Thomas Merton

WRITING THE BETTER STORY

1. Write about your enemy—real or imaginary.
2. What practical steps can you take today to love an enemy?

DAY TWENTY-EIGHT
STRETCHING

"Stretch out your hand."
–Mark 3:5

A few paragraphs into Walter Wink's autobiography, he shares a story about being part of a worship service where the facilitators focused on the story of the man with the withered hand. Wink, a theologian and thinker who had a keen interest in understanding the intersection of the world of "principalities and powers" with issues of social justice, influenced me greatly during my college years. I had not read anything from him in a few decades.

As the Gospel story goes, Jesus enters the synagogue and bumps into a man with a withered hand. It happened to be the Sabbath—a day celebrated within the Jewish tradition when people were not supposed to work. But like many good ideas that were designed to really help people, the bigger picture gets lost. The rule becomes the big picture. Or, as some say, the tail begins to wag the dog. Or the finger that is supposed to direct our attention to the bigger idea actually becomes the idea itself and the object of our attention.

Predictably, there is a posse of small men, with small hearts, who have a need to assert their control and power. So, they watch Jesus with the kind of narrow focus that looks for the flaw. Jesus does not disappoint. He plays into their hand. Jesus knows that the bigger picture is to bring this man to fullness, to make him whole and fully alive. This is the bigger picture of the Sabbath—a day of rest given to humanity so humans can renew themselves. Jesus calls the man to participate in his own healing. "Stretch out your hand," he says.

And the response of the Pharisees is predictable. It is the response of small men, with small hearts, worried about trying to control their small universes. Immediately they leave the scene and find some likeminded friends and begin to conspire around destroying Jesus.

So, at this particular worship service Wink was asked: What is your withered hand? What part of your being is dead?

The group members were given a piece of clay, asked to close their eyes and create something that resembles a picture of who they are. In the silence and solitude of the moment, Wink closed his eyes and began to form a bird. It was a bird poised to fly but had a broken wing. Then he tried to understand what it meant. Wink determined that his broken wing symbolized his lack of feelings. That "withered" part of himself was the inability to feel.

"Stretch out your hand," says Jesus. He asks for participation, for action. The man does not heal his own hand, but he must take some initiative. He's called to do something.

For the next six months, Wink decided, he must write down things he feels. Sometimes there was nothing. Sometimes there were many feelings. Sometimes just one. But his act of "stretching" meant simply writing down what he felt. And in writing down the things he felt, Wink began to find healing.

I wonder how many of us, especially men, can relate to Wink's self-revelation. I know I can. My wife often asks me how I feel. I can honestly respond that I don't really feel anything. Feelings are difficult for me. Or maybe it's a fear to be vulnerable. Maybe I have some stretching to do…some interior work to complete. Maybe my feelings are the "hand" that needs to be stretched.

The words of Brene Brown, who has researched the value and impact of

Day Twenty-Eight: Stretching

vulnerability in a person's life, challenge me as well. Vulnerability, she argues, is linked to love. And love is what makes us whole. Love makes our lives whole. Love helps God write a better story.

She writes, "To love someone fiercely, to believe in something with your whole heart, to celebrate a fleeting moment in time, to fully engage in a life that doesn't come with guarantees—these are the risks that involve vulnerability and often pain. But I'm learning that recognizing and leaning into the discomfort of vulnerability teaches us how to live with joy, gratitude and grace."[55]

Just as the man with the withered hand needed to respond to Jesus' challenge in order for his story to become more complete, we are asked to do the same. *Stretch.* Stretch. Stretch! It means something different for each of us during different seasons of our lives.

REFLECTION:

> "One life on this earth is all that we get, whether it is enough or not enough, and the obvious conclusion would seem to be that at the very least we are fools if we do not live it as fully and bravely and beautifully as we can."
> –Frederick Buechner

WRITING THE BETTER STORY

1. What's your broken wing? Your withered hand?
2. What part of your life do you need to "stretch out to Jesus"?

DAY TWENTY-NINE
WHERE ARE THE OAKS?

"May I be alive when I die."
–D.W. Winnicott

Once upon a time, in a not-so-faraway land, there was a kingdom of acorns, nestled at the foot of a grand old oak tree. Since the citizens of this kingdom were modern, fully Westernized acorns, they went about their business with purposeful energy; and since they were midlife, baby boomer acorns, they engaged in a lot of self-help courses. There were seminars called, "Getting All You Can out of Your Shell" and "Seven Habits of Highly Effective Acorns." There were woundedness and recovery groups for acorns who had been bruised in their original fall from the tree. There were spas for oiling and polishing those shells and various acornopathic therapies to enhance longevity and well-being.

One day in midst of this kingdom, there suddenly appeared a knotty little stranger, dropped out of the blue by a passing bird. He was capless and dirty, making an immediate negative impression on his fellow acorns. And crouched beneath the oak tree, he stammered out a wild tale. Pointing upward at the tree, he said, "We…are…that!"

"Delusional," laughed one acorn. Another mockingly queried, "So tell us, how would we become that tree?"

"Well," said he, pointing downward, "it has something to do with going into the ground…and cracking open our shell."

"That's insane," chorused the group in full throttled unison. "Totally morbid!" "If we did that," scoffed another, "We wouldn't be acorns anymore."

The acorn story isn't original. Like many preachers, I'm a scavenger… always looking for a good story, a powerful metaphor or an example that leads to a deeper truth. So I took a few liberties and modified this old parable—and I think it's a jewel. Like any good parable, it lands a different meaning on each of us. You've probably made your determination. Here's mine:

I've always believed that authentic faith should lead people to become better and more complete versions of themselves. Each of us is a unique masterpiece, made in the image of God. For numerous reasons this image gets lost and fades. God's great promise and gift is our restoration—bringing vibrancy, radiance and aliveness to our divine imprint. An early church father, Irenaeus of Lyon, captured it beautifully: "The glory of God is a human fully alive." Our aliveness as human beings can be metaphorically imagined in the process of an acorn becoming an oak tree. Acorns are wonderful—but God's vision for our lives is so much fuller.

Yet there's a problem. This journey to fullness can't be purchased like a seven-day, all-expense-paid Disney cruise. And sadly, we can't just read our way to this place, retreat our way to this place, pray our way to this place, or even church our way to this place. As the chipped and broken acorn audaciously suggests, "It has something to do with going into the ground." And that idea is a little morbid—especially in a culture that increasingly builds its identity, vision and values around the promotion of self.

But for those who desire to begin this journey of transformation, the word often used is …surrender. Surrender begins by letting go of our little selves: those primal needs to control, to win, and to dominate. Surrender means letting go of our norms and our preferences and even beliefs that limit transformation. Surrender means releasing those thoughts and ideas that bind us as acorns for a lifetime.

Day Twenty-Nine: Where Are the Oaks?

Jesus said it this way: "Whoever would save his life shall lose it, and whoever shall lose his life for my sake will save it" (Luke 9:24). It's a little countercultural, isn't it? Or how about this zinger: "Unless a grain of wheat falls into the ground and dies, it remains a single grain, but if it dies, it shall yield a rich harvest" (John 12:24). Jesus modeled and taught surrender. Even the apostle Paul noticed that Jesus "emptied himself and took on the form of a servant." Self-emptying births a fuller life. Less of *me* means more of God.

So I might argue that this current historical moment offers a unique gift. Our lives are currently being disrupted, disturbed and disoriented. Old ways of thinking are being challenged. Routines are being broken. Assumptions dismantled. But here's the truth: there's an opportunity to let go of some old baggage and be filled with something new. Yes, the path can be uncomfortable. Deep change has a cost.

Theologian Cynthia Bourgeault says it this way "...in any situation in life, confronted by an outer threat or opportunity, you can notice yourself responding inwardly in one or two ways. Either you will brace, harden, and resist, or you will soften, open, and yield."[56]

She continues by saying, "If you go with your former gesture, you will be catapulted immediately into your smaller self, with its animal instincts and survival responses. If you stay with the latter regardless of the outer conditions, you will remain in alignment with your innermost being, and through it..."

In other words, God can reach you.

"Soften, open and yield," are the words challenging me today. If I find myself bracing, hardening and resisting...I need to ask: *why?* I need to take inventory. I need to reflect and go deeper. And hopefully I'll find myself praying: "Dear Lord, help me surrender and trust your mysterious work which always wants to reorder my life in ways I can't begin to imagine."

I've met an Oak or two in my day. They are special people for sure—

humble, graceful, compassionate, wise, generous, joyful, kind and… fully alive. They've all taken the journey—a journey marked with surrender, a journey that "cracked the shell," took them "into the ground" and brought them back to us as magnificent examples of what it means to be fully human. As beautiful Oaks in our midst, they continually remind us "we…are…that."[57]

REFLECTION

> "Creativity and newness of life have a cost, and the cost is what appears to look like death. But really it is not. It is just letting go of one thing to make room for another thing. Loss is always perceived as an enemy or affliction, and looks like what we don't want. Somehow to embrace loss, spiritually speaking, is to achieve something more and something bigger. Some form of positive dying invariably allows us to be united with what is Larger Reality, but of course we never know that ahead of time. So if you spend your whole life avoiding dying, the spiritual teachers would say you will never get there. Meditate on the phrase Jesus gave us: 'Unless the grain of wheat dies, it remains just a grain of wheat; but if it dies, it bears much fruit' (John 12:24). That quotation is about as counterintuitive as you can get. Rationally I cannot prove that to you. You have to walk through it. You have to experience it to know that it is in fact true and *true for you*. Frankly, none of us go there until we are shoved."[58]
>
> –Richard Rohr

WRITING THE BETTER STORY

1. What's something which you need to "let go"?
2. In what ways do you limit yourself to being an "acorn", when God wants you to be an oak? Write down a few examples.

DAY THREE
GRATITUDE JOURNALS

"Gratitude is joy, and gratitude is justice."
–Diana Butler Bass

"Please send me a copy of your paper," I asked with a genuine sense of curiosity. "I really want to read it."

"Come on Dad," with a less than enthusiastic reply. "You know you'll just critique it."

My youngest daughter Madeline started a Master of Divinity program a few years ago. Admittedly, I'm a little excited and find myself vicariously reliving my seminary days through her—asking about the books she's reading, discussing lectures…and wanting to read her papers.

"I won't critique it," I promised. "Just want to see what you're writing." Wink. Wink.

So the paper arrived. Voraciously I began to read her epistle—something about pastoral counseling and the act of listening. Halfway into the second page I noticed a couple of lines about a family dinner tradition.

"My father would bring out the gratitude journal no matter who was at the dinner table," she wrote. She then described how everyone was required to share something for which they were grateful. "In my younger years it was boring and awkward," she confessed. "Especially when we had friends over."

Now a 30-year old graduate student reflecting more deeply on her life, Madeline concluded: "Engaging in the gratitude journal practice made us more attentive, accepting where we were at that moment, and more observant of our thoughts and feelings." I paused to reread those words. Wait…what? My rebellious youngest child remembered the gratitude journal?

Those who have experienced the blessing (and challenges) of raising children I'm sure can relate. Despite the demands on our time, financial pressures, aging parents for whom we must care, marriages that need nurture, and civic commitments requiring our duty—we try our best, hope and pray that a few of the good things we did for our children stick. The gratitude journal ritual was one that took root!

I say ritual because in our family, the journal found its way to the dinner table regardless of the current circumstances. Gratitude was part of our nightly rhythm. A bad day at school? We journaled. An argument with my wife about a credit card bill five minutes before dinner? We journaled. A tough loss on the soccer pitch? A crisis at work…we stopped, reflected, looked for the good and journaled together.

Robert Emmons, who studies gratitude at UC Davis, makes a similar argument. "And this is what grateful people do. They have learned to transform adversity into opportunity no matter what happens, to see existence itself as a gift." The late Catholic theologian Henri Nouwen said it another way, "Gratitude rarely comes without real effort. The more we choose gratitude in the ordinary places of our day, the easier it becomes."

Despite the incredible challenges of life, I still believe there's an opportunity to pull out the gratitude journal. Let's choose to discover things for which we can be grateful. In no way am I saying to sugarcoat life. There is real grief, real pain, real disappointment. But let's push a little deeper and be intentional about seeing the good, pausing and thanking God.

Day Thirty: Gratitude Journals

REFLECTION

> "History attests that religion and religious people tend to be narrow. Instead of expanding our capacity for life, joy, and mystery, religion often contracts it. As systematic theology advances, the sense of wonder declines."[59]
> —Brennan Manning, Abba's Child
>
> "I'm one of the blessed ones. I get paid—highly—for being myself and for doing what I most enjoy: sharing ideas with other people. I live a big life. But in reality, it's the small things that fill me up. I sliced a fresh peach today that was so sweet, so succulent, so divinely peachy that even as I was eating it, I thought, there *are no words to adequately describe this peach—one has to taste it to understand the true definition of peachiness.* I closed my eyes, the better to feel the flavor. Even that wasn't enough, though, so I saved the last two bites to share with Stedman, to see if he affirmed my assessment of best peach ever. He took the first bite and said, 'Mmm, mmm, mmm…this peach reminds me of childhood.' And so that small thing got bigger, as all things do when shared in a spirit of appreciation."[60]
> —Oprah Winfrey

WRITING THE BETTER STORY

> 1. List ten "small" things for which you are grateful for today.
> 2. How does gratitude make us "bigger" people? Are there ways your religion has made you smaller?

DAY THIRTY-ONE
IS SOCIAL JUSTICE BIBLICAL?

"Be living signs of God's merciful love."
–Pope Francis

"...I am also pretty sure that the words social justice are not in the Bible," revealed the email. "And therefore, it's not biblical."

When I read my friends words this past week, it reminded me of a story I heard years ago by an urban ministry pioneer named Ray Bakke. Ray was speaking at a suburban church outside of Chicago, sharing about his work with inner-city youth—job training, tutoring, athletic programs. After he spoke, a gentleman approached him: "Rev Bakke, it sounds like you're committed to promoting a social gospel," he said with a slight tone of judgment. "How does the true Gospel fit into your mission?"

Pastor Bakke paused for a minute. "Can I ask you a question?" "Sure," replied the man.

"I'm curious, where do you and your family live?"

The gentleman named an affluent, tree-lined street in a suburban town outside Chicago.

"Why do you live there?" continued Bakke.

"Great schools," volunteered the man. "I travel a lot for work, so I feel my wife and children are safe. A terrific public library. The parks are beautiful as well."

"I find it fascinating," replied Bakke. "And I'm not judging you for selecting your neighborhood. But the reasons you've cited for living in your community are all social—education, safety, public services. You spend the bulk of your resources and life energy maintaining these social supports. At the risk of being blunt, I really think you're the one committed to a social gospel."

I forget how the story ends. The two men may have continued to argue into the wee hours of the morning. Or maybe the gentleman became a regular donor to Bakke's ministry. To me, the conversation reveals the stark differences between ministry in more affluent communities and ministry in under-resourced communities. In affluent settings, many of the social needs of people—good schools, sports leagues, community safety, jobs, nice parks—are provided, which allow churches to focus exclusively on "spiritual issues." In under resourced communities, these social supports simply don't exist. Since humans are not one-dimensional spiritual beings, social issues must be considered if ministry is to be transformative.

My friend who questioned whether the term social justice is biblical, was ultimately concerned that we were teaching a "social justice" class to our teens this summer. I'm glad he raised the question. I'm also glad he didn't walk away from our ministry. A conversation was requested. I complied. We had a lively and informative exchange.

In my experience we Christians tend to gravitate towards different "camps"—like- minded groups of people whose theology and politics align with others who hold similar beliefs. One camp of Christians may feel their primary job is to get people saved so they can enjoy eternal life with God in heaven. "Jesus is the only thing that matters," I hear frequently—implying that the social conditions in which people live are of secondary concern to the eternal glory awaiting beyond the grave. Harsh realities of daily life are to be endured because we're "just

Day Thirty-One: Is Social Justice Biblical?

passing through." Jesus is Savior only—not a man who lived, taught, spoke truth to power and cared for the physical lives of real people. This group might argue that it's important to be charitable, but challenging systems that create adverse conditions is not in the Jesus playbook.

Another "camp" of Christians feels that the social conditions in which humans live their lives, and the systems that create them—poverty, violence, racism, systemic injustices—need to be challenged and made more just. After all, Christians are agents of God's witness and need to play an active role in advancing this realm of peace and justice on earth "as it is in heaven." Humans are made in the *imago Dei*—the image of God. Anything that damages or hurts this "image" needs to be confronted and changed. Life on earth matters. God wants human beings to flourish now—body, mind, and spirit.

So where does that leave us? Should we be teaching our kids about social justice, or should a Christian ministry be focusing simply on the spiritual dimensions of life?

I find myself returning to the Bible during these conversations, fully acknowledging that my interpretation of scripture is biased and influenced by my history, education and the context in which I read it. But even with my bias, it's hard to overlook the 2,000 references to justice and poverty in the Bible. Digging deeper into these verses reveals a startling truth: many verses pertain to the social conditions of human beings! The book of Leviticus is all about the law—right and fair living between people. Scripture speaks out against "corrupt scales" in the marketplace (commerce), exploiting the poor by charging exorbitant interest rates (usury), acquiring multiple properties at the expense of the poor (unjust housing), exploiting widows and orphans (misuse of power), welcoming aliens and treating them well (immigration) paying day laborers fairly and quickly (good management) …It's all in there! God seems to care about the nitty gritty details of human life. So, if the Bible is true, social realities *are* a concern to God.

And what about Jesus? Was he concerned only with the spiritual dimensions of people's life, or was he concerned about the social and physical dimensions as well? Jesus healed people (health), he fed people (physical wellbeing), he embraced the outcast and crossed racial/ethnic barriers (advocacy) and he defended women and children in a culture where it was not popular. Jesus also spoke harshly against those who hid behind their religious practices while they "…neglected the weightier matters of the law: justice, mercy and faith" (Matthew 23:23). It appears that Jesus practiced the social dimensions of justice.

So why have the words "social justice" become so politicized and divisive for Christians? A memorable quote by Archbishop Dom Helder Camara highlights our divergent perspectives:

> "When I feed the poor, they call me a Saint, but when I ask why the poor are hungry, they call me a communist."

As Christians, we tend to be much more comfortable with the concept of charity than justice, probably because our solutions of fixing injustice look so different for each of us. Research does reveal that Christians are some of most generous people—hands down. But discussing injustice can make us uncomfortable—perhaps because addressing root causes can demand more than writing a check and, at times, reveal our own complicity in an injustice…calling us to do some soul searching.

I've always believed that Christians can't avoid addressing root causes that keep youth and families in cycles of perpetual poverty. I believe we need to be equipping young people to live the abundant lives that Jesus promised. Charity has its place, just as an emergency room is critical at a hospital. But long-term health calls us to look at factors making unhealthy people. To get to this place, Christians must move beyond political and doctrinal differences and stay focused on what really matters—preparing the whole child to live into the fullness of who God create them to be.

So my friend is actually correct. He wins the argument. The literal words "social justice" do not appear in the Bible (at least I can't find them). But the biblical commands to be "doers of justice" and "minister justice to the poor and needy" certainly compels me to understanding, confronting and acting out their social implications. In some circles, our different perspectives might signal the end of our relationship. United as brothers and sisters in Christ, I'm hoping the journey of creating a better world is just beginning.

REFLECTION

> "Jesus did not die at the hands of muggers, rapists, or thugs. He fell into the well-scrubbed hands of deeply religious people—societies most respected leaders."[61]
> —Brennen Manning

> "What I want is mercy, not sacrifice."
> —Hosea 6:6

> "We serve the world by being spiritually well. The first question is not, 'How much do we do?' or 'How many people do we help out?' but 'Are we interiorly at peace?' The distinction between contemplation and action can be misleading. Jesus' action flowed from his interior communion with God. His presence was healing, and it changed the world. In a sense he didn't do anything! 'Everyone who touched him was healed.'"[62]
> —Henri Nouwan

> "We are afraid of religion because it interprets rather than just observes. Religion does not confirm that there are hungry people in the world; it interprets the hungry to be our brethren who we are allowed to serve."[63]
> —Dorothy Soelle

WRITING THE BETTER STORY

1. What does "doing justice" mean to you?
2. How might you cultivate and interior life that birth's life, healing and justice for others?

DAY THIRTY-TWO
BEAUTIFUL MOMENTS

"Everything can be taken from a person but one thing, the last of the human freedoms—to choose one's attitude in any given set of circumstances, to choose one's own way."
–Viktor Frankl, *Man's Search for Meaning*

"It was our last beautiful moment together," whispered my old friend. "It's a memory I hold onto—it gets me through my lonely days."

Then he described his "beautiful moment" in minute detail. New Year's Eve the previous year. As a couple in their early 90's, the days of going to Galas and watching the ball drop in Times Square were long behind them. After 61 years of marriage, a fun night was turning on the gas fireplace, watching Muffin the house cat curl up on their laps and having a few sips of Sherry.

"Our son was visiting from New York," continued Bill. "He sat down at our old family piano and started playing Sinatra's, Come Fly with Me. One of our favorites."

And then Bill and Rita started to dance. Just the two of them—shuffling in circles across the living room carpet, embracing one another and laughing like high school sweethearts. The music continued: Nat King Cole, When I Fall in Love. Sam Cook, You Send Me. With each lyric a memory of earlier days filled their minds—their first meeting, their first dance, their first kiss, their years of life together.

"A day later Rita suffered a stroke," recounted Bill. "That night was our last beautiful moment together."

For different reasons conversations stick with me. It might have something to do with the particular moment, a word shared, a moment of sobering honesty. But I've never been able to shake the image of Bill and Rita experiencing their last beautiful moment together. It got me thinking about the moments I miss—a stark reminder that the only thing guaranteed is the present moment.

Simone Weil, the French mystic, once wrote that prayer is simply "coming to attention". Her French forbearer, Blaise Pascal felt that the greatest enemy to the spiritual life was inattention—drowsiness, complacency, and what he called the "Gethsemane sleep." I believe Jesus spent a lot of his time trying to get his followers to wake up, to be present in the moment and to always be on the lookout for ordinary people reflecting the heart of God in real time.

In the humdrum of daily life, Jesus had the knack of drawing our attention to the widow for her generosity, the leper for his gratitude, the anointing woman at Bethany for her lavish love, the tax collector for his contrition, the bleeding woman for her courage… Jesus essentially calls our attention to beautiful, sacred, and redemptive moments that fill the ordinary spaces of life and says, "Notice". I call it spotting the sacred.

A lot of people are feeling the heaviness of our historical moment. It's easy to diet on cynicism, negatively, division and the despair pervading our country right now. I'm not denying these elements exist—and, like you, I feel it deeply. But we also have a choice to decide what gets our attention and feeds our soul. As people of God, we need to dig to deeper levels of awareness and consciousness. We need to move beyond simply satisfying our spiritual thirst with surface water—drilling into the subterranean depths where God's living water is found.

Look for, ponder and dwell on these things, writes Saint Paul. What are these things? *Whatever is true, whatever is right, whatever is pure, what-*

ever is lovely, whatever is admirable, whatever is excellent or praiseworthy. (Philippians 4:18)

Sounds like a clarion call to discover more beautiful moments—moments that will refresh, renew, challenge and revive our spirits for the journey ahead.

REFLECTION

"In the entire history of the universe, let alone in your own history, there has never been another day just like today, and there will never be another just like it again. Today is the point to which all your yesterdays have been leading since the hour of your birth. It is the point from which all your tomorrows will proceed until the hour of your death. If you were aware of how precious today is, you could hardly live through it. Unless you are aware of how precious it is, you can hardly be said to be living at all."[64]

–Frederick Buechner

WRITING THE BETTER STORY

1. Write down one beautiful moment from the last few days. What made it beautiful?
2. Ponder today. Think about each moment, each encounter…each breath you were allowed to take. Take a moment to write down words of thanks.

DAY THIRTY-THREE
SAINTS IN OUR MIDST

> *"In his holy flirtation with the world, God occasionally drops a handkerchief. These handkerchiefs are called saints."*
> –Frederick Buechner

"Do you have a minute?"

I was in full stride to my next meeting, focused and completely oblivious to the woman quickly approaching me on the right and trying to get my attention. A few feet from colliding, I noticed a blurred movement in my peripheral, turned my head to see a familiar smiling face.

"Hey Dolores," I called. "How you doing?"

"I just want to thank you," she gushed. "For giving me the best Thanksgiving ever."

"But I haven't seen you since the break?" I volleyed. "I don't think I can take any credit for your Thanksgiving."

"Sure you can," she replied "You and your team have given me a chance to share what I love to do—teach piano to children. For that I'm eternally thankful."

And teach she did. Week in, week out. Dolores set up shop in the only unused space on campus during the 3pm-6pm hours—the busy hallway outside our after-school program area. We'd roll out the piano from storage every Tuesday and Thursday afternoon and our children lined up for their 20-minute private lesson with Ms. Dolores.

A beautiful image. Pandemonium and noise swirling around the makeshift studio—Dolores and her eager students focused and oblivious to anything but the black and white keys in front of them. Notes and chords were taught, finger work modeled, and rudimentary forms of sight reading introduced. Humbling teaching conditions didn't matter. Dolores just loved to share her gift. And that made her Thanksgiving holiday "the best."

Sadly that was Dolores' last Thanksgiving. She passed away a few months ago from an unexpected and swift battle with cancer. One of Dolores' last conscious acts was listening to a recording of our April all-staff meeting. Collectively, our community prayed and thanked her for the joy she brought so many of our children. It makes me smile to think she slipped out of consciousness and into eternity being praised for her generous spirit.

These are the heroes who drift through our campus each week. They ask for nothing, don't desire headlines and would be embarrassed to be publicly recognized. They pay for their own gas, ask for no reimbursements, and sacrifice their most precious commodity—time. Sharing what they must give—their hearts, their talents and their love to children—with kids they don't really know. Humble, sincere, authentic, and selfless are words that come to my mind.

Their volunteerism is often an extension of their faith—faith in God, faith in the potential of children, and faith in the power of love. I'm convinced it's the Dolores' of the world who make our country great. They're the glue who holds us together. As the barker's bark, the dividers divide and the hurters hurt, the Dolores' quietly move beneath the tumultuous surface of our society mending hurts, calming fears, and sowing seeds of peace and beauty. These are the true patriots who live and breathe "liberty and justice for all" through their words and deeds.

We find these characters in scripture as well. They are the unsung heroes

Day Thirty-Three: Saints in Our Midst

who show up when everyone else has moved on. They are the people who keep the God story moving in the right direction, despite the overwhelming odds. Like Mary at the tomb—grief-stricken because the body of her friend has vanished—she ends up transforming a moment of despair into the greatest message of hope the world has ever heard: "I have seen the Lord," becomes Mary's first sermon as the first preacher of the Christian movement—and she's still quoted today.

"When all the other disciples are fleeing, Mary Magdalene stands firm," notices theologian Cynthia Bourgeault. "She does not run; she does not betray or lie about her commitment; she witnesses. Hers is clearly a demonstration of either the deepest human love or the highest spiritual understanding of what Jesus was teaching, perhaps both."[65]

"We must also keep our eyes open for the saints of our own culture," adds the Episcopalian priest Charles Hoffacker, "Their witness will be close enough to our concerns, or what should be our concerns, to leave us uncomfortable with our spiritual compromises." And that's why we must notice the Dolores' who float in and out of our lives. They call us to become our better selves.

So rest in peace, my friend. Thanks for being a living reminder of what it means to serve with joy. May your heavenly music studio have a well-tuned Steinway and be filled with the laughter of children discovering their first Sonata.

REFLECTION

> "We are called upon to do something new, to confront a no man's land, to push into a forest where there are no well-worn paths and from which no one has returned to guide us. This is what the existentialists call *the anxiety of nothingness*. To live into the future means to leap into the unknown, and this requires a degree of courage for which there is no immediate precedent and which few people realize."[66]
>
> –Rollo May

"If you think you are too small to be effective you have never been in bed with a mosquito."

—Bette Reese

WRITING THE BETTER STORY

1. Is there a saint in your midst? Write a few sentences about that individual. What can you learn from them?
2. What gift would you like to share with the world?

DAY THIRTY-FOUR
HABIT OF HOPE

> *"Always be prepared to give an answer to everyone who asks you to give the reason for the hope that you have. But do this with gentleness and respect."*
> —1 Peter 3:15

"What's the building over there?" I pointed across the dusty field to a weathered cinder block structure.

"That's our temporary boy's dorm," responded my host, "Used to be an old gas station."

Curiosity got the better of me. I started to walk towards the compound, wanting to witness the living conditions firsthand.

So far my visit to Malawi—the small sub-Saharan country wedged between Mozambique and Zambia—had been encouraging. I was able to witness some of remarkable work created by Malawian leaders who had trained with our organization over the years—leaders who returned to their home countries to start similar youth serving organizations. That day's visit was to Rise Malawi Ministries where two dynamic leaders birthed a high school in a remote and impoverished community.

"How many boys living here?" I queried.

"Eighteen," replied their principal. "We weren't supposed to house any boys, but kids heard about the school from surrounding villages and started traveling for hours each day. This was our only option. We rent the building for $40 a month."

I pushed open the door, stepped inside and quickly withdrew. A pungent odor seared my nostrils. My abrupt retreat was noticed.

"We had bats in the rafters," apologized my host. "We've gotten rid of them—just not the smell."

Needless to say, I was dismayed by the conditions. I was embarrassed to think we had students living in this space. Yet something had caught my eye—words scribbled on the ceiling tile above a bunk bed in the back right corner. I took a deep breath and re-entered the building. Inching closer and closer to the bunk bed, I strained my eyes to read the words written with a chalk-like substance. Pushing aside the green netting, used to protect the boys from malaria-carrying mosquitoes, I read:

"Life is 10% what happens to you and 90% how you respond."

What? The words seemed out of place. To read them on an inspirational poster at the local Planet Fitness might fit. But seeing them scratched on ceiling tiles, in cramped and poorly ventilated living conditions, created a kind of cognitive dissonance.

The student occupying the top bunk obviously wrote the message for himself. A daily reminder—the last thing he'd read before he drifted off to sleep, and the first thing to greet his eyes in the morning.

I imagined it might be his little prayer—a rosary so to speak—a daily ritual helping him find the right mental space to deal with the obstacles confronting him. Where he discovered the quote, I'll never know.

I've learned during my life that memorable life lessons often are discovered unexpectedly. They sneak up—finding us when we least expect it. A bolt of lightning might have made a lesser impact on me. Words

Day Thirty-Four: Habit of Hope

that would lose their agency in most locations took on a sacramental quality. A fourteen-year-old boy, growing up in debilitating poverty, reminding himself daily that he has still has a choice. It was a message I needed to hear.

My seminary professor, Lewis Smedes, used to tell us the "hope is a habit" and "hopeful people take responsibility for their hoping." He would continue by saying, "choosing to keep on struggling against despair and to keep on choosing for hope—that is to take responsibly for our hoping." Smedes' words were always close. But the boy in the back bunk obviously learned this lesson without a seminary degree. A "habit of hope" was being quietly cultivated.

"You wouldn't happen to know the student that sleeps there?" I asked the principal as we walked back towards the school. I felt compelled to meet the young man whose idea of "graffiti" was my writing inspirational quotes on ceiling tiles.

The school's principal stopped and surveyed the hundreds of students moving around the dusty campus. He finally pointed to a young man reading under a tree next to a classroom block. "That's him. Over there."

"Excuse me?" I inquired as I got within a few feet. "Are you the young man who sleeps on the upper back bunk bed—the one who wrote the quote in the ceiling tile?"

For a moment he paused—maybe thinking he was about to be scolded. Slowly he nodded.

"What's your name?" I beckoned.

"My name...my name," he slowly stammered in broken English... "my name is Hope."

Hope? What are the odds? Out of 400 students attending the school, the one young man I needed to thank for giving me a needed reminder... his name...*Hope*.

"Well Hope," I affirmed with a smile and handshake. "I appreciate you leaving a message for me to read today."

After chatting a few minutes about his dreams and aspirations, I said goodbye and walked back to my waiting car thinking… *my habit of hope begins today.*

P.S. The following year a new dormitory was built for the boys at Rise Malawi. A woman in Chambersburg, Pennsylvania heard about the bats and decided to do something. There are now 80 boys staying on campus. And there are no bats!

REFLECTION

> "Jesus said, 'Live ecstatically. Move out of that place of death and toward life because I am the God who is living. Wherever I am, there is life, there is change, there is growth, there is increase and blossoming and something new. I am going to make everything new."
>
> "For us to dare to live a life in which we continue to move out of the static places and take trusting steps in new directions—that is what faith is all about. The Greek word for faith means to trust—to trust that the ground before you that you never walked on is safe ground, God's ground, holy ground."[67]
>
> –Henri Nouwan

Day Thirty-Four: Habit of Hope

> "O Lord, open my eyes that I may see the need of others, open my ears that I may hear their cries, open my heart so that they need not be without succor, let me be not afraid to defend the weak because of the anger of the rich. Show me where love and hope and faith are needed and used me to bring them to those places. And so, open my eyes and my ears that I may this coming day be able to do some work of peace for Thee."
>
> –Dag Hammarskjold

WRITING THE BETTER STORY

1. How have you chosen the habit of hope today?
2. Write a little about the new thing God is doing in you. What is it? What is it like?

DAY THIRTY-FIVE
A FEW GOOD BRICKS

"Without heroes, we're all plain people and don't know how far we can go."
–Bernard Malamud, *The Natural*

"Where would you like to go to lunch?" I asked the petite, silver haired woman in the passenger seat. "It's my treat. This is a big day—sky's the limit."

Not every day a son gets to buy his mother lunch on her 88th birthday. So, I was all in—especially after traveling 3,000 miles to be there—even making sure my credit card hadn't exceeded its limit. After all, she might pick the Four Seasons. Maybe Ruth Chris' SteakHouse. No worries. I was ready to splurge.

"Could we get a cheeseburger," she demurred softly. "McDonalds, okay?"

At this stage I've learned not to argue with my mother about issues that make no rational sense—this was one of those moments. No attempt would be made to upgrade to Olive Garden or even Denny's. If mom wanted a Cheeseburger at McDonalds…it's the Golden Arches.

Noticing the "dining room" closed, I pulled into the drive through lane. Rats! No plastic seats and sticky tables this year. "Can I take your order?" crackled the voice through the loudspeaker. Words almost out of my mouth, I felt a tug on my sleeve.

"Could I get a Vanilla shake as well?" she giggled with childlike excitement.

At that moment I would have "super-sized" her meal for an extra 59 cents. But I didn't want her eating warmed over French fries the rest of the week—she would insist on taking leftovers home. A small cheeseburger, a milkshake, and a Hertz rental car would be the ambianic ingredients for this celebratory meal. We drove off to find a quiet space.

"Tell me about a memorable birthday?" I queried with curiosity as we nibbled on fries and watched the Seagulls scavenge across the parking lot for their noon day meal. And mom, being mom, reminded me about growing up in the shadows of the Great Depression, the scarcity of resources and the fond memory that a really good birthday meant getting a bottle of Fanta and a Nickel to buy some penny candy at the local Five and Dime. Something beautifully simple about it all—a reminder Chucky Cheese themed parties aren't really needed to create rich and lasting memories.

This past week our staff discussed the theme of healthy life foundations. After watching horrific images of people losing their homes to hurricanes and feeling the turbulent winds of our current reality relentlessly beating against the retaining walls of our daily norms, a conversation around foundations seemed like a relevant topic. Many feel their foundations are being shaken.

A question surfaced: what kind of foundation does a person really need to weather the storms of life and flourish as human beings made in the image of God? A second: And how do we create these foundations for ourselves and the children we serve?

As a community we talked about our parent's contribution to our foundations—a powerful conversation revealing the connection between what our parents modeled and its lasting impact on our faith, our sense of family, our desire to serve and our desire to leave the world a better place. I'm grateful for my mother's faith and frugality (my wife not so grateful for the second f-word)—a frugality allowing her to share

Day Thirty-Five: A Few Good Bricks

generously with those in need.

And for those in our community who've spent years healing from dysfunctional and broken families, they shared their challenges rebuilding life foundations, how following God has helped and how they're living differently for their own children.

Of course, Jesus was mentioned in our conversations. After his famous Sermon on the Mount, Jesus shares a timeless parable about wise and foolish builders. Wise builders, he argues, "hear my words" and "put them into practice." Conversely, foolish builders hear the words but never take the time to do the hard work of implementation. Foolish builders take shortcuts. Foundation building always involves intentionality and the practice of behaviors the public seldom sees.

So, what are these "words" that Jesus wants us to hear and practice for foundation building? Let me share "a few good bricks" from Matthew's gospel: "Store up for yourselves treasures in heaven, where moth and rust do not destroy…" Essentially invest in things that matter—things possessing eternal value (6:19) "Do not worry about tomorrow…each day has enough trouble of its own."(6:34) Be present to the moment. Don't dwell in the past, don't fear the future. Be attentive to the now. "So, in everything, do to others what you would have them do to you…". (7:12) No explanation really needed. Think of the 100 ways you can implement the Golden Rule each day.

Add these good bricks to your life foundation and let the winds howl. When the storm passes, you'll still be standing and have a testimony to share.

REFLECTION

"You are a child of God. Your playing small doesn't serve the world. There is nothing enlightened about shrinking so that others won't feel insecure around you. We were born to make manifest the glory of God within us. It's not just in some of us; it's in everyone. As we are liberated from our own fear, our presence automatically liberates others."[68]
–Marianne Williamson

"In the spiritual life there are no tricks and no short cuts… One cannot begin to face the real difficulties of the life of prayer and meditation unless one is first perfectly content to be a beginner and really experience oneself as one who knows little or nothing, and has a desperate need to learn the bare rudiments. Those who think they 'know' from the beginning never, in fact, come to know anything…we do not want to be beginners. But let us be convinced of the fact that we will never be anything else but beginners, all our life."[69]
–Thomas Merton

"A successful person is one who can build a foundation with the bricks that others throw at them."
–David Brinkley

WRITING THE BETTER STORY

1. Recall a storm you have faced. What were some of the foundational elements of your life that gave you a sense of stability and hope?

2. Write about "one good brick" you would like to integrate more deeply into your life.

DAY THIRTY-SIX
OPEN TABLE

"We do not think ourselves into a new way of living, we live our way into a new way of thinking."
–Richard Rohr

"Thank you for this article," read my early evening email of October 20th. "I also now have Hope in my heart."

Sadly, that was the last note I received from my friend.

Deb passed away suddenly, much to the shock of her husband Bill, of 46 years, and the beautiful family they faithfully nurtured together. Death is always difficult. Losing a spouse, parent, friend abruptly is disorienting. No time for last words, hugs or goodbyes. Her last email to me was never answered. That's a regret I'll live with.

If Deb's life embodied one theme, it was abundant encouragement and extravagant hospitality. I received both from her, frequently. In a society too busy to sit and eat together, Deb and Bill instituted a memorable ritual years ago. Every Monday night—emphasis on EVERY—the front door of their Hickory Lane home was left ajar, and an open dinner table awaited any wanderer. No RSVPs needed. No Google calendar to confirm if it was happening. No phone call necessary to invite the Texan uncle unexpectedly swinging through town. No cancellation polices. No basket on the table for a donation. Just show up ...with appetite. Monday night: 6 p.m. Food, fellowship, and your soul graced by the radical gift of inclusive table fellowship.

Sometimes eight guests straggled through the door, other times 14 arrived together, sometimes 30 wafted in and out over the 2-hour window. A widow next door. An executive in town for business. A graduate student needing a break from peanut butter and crackers. A coworker recently divorced and lonely. A first-time visitor to church. Eclectic and unpredictable people. Dinner was at times quiet and intimate, but more often chaotic and noisy. The food was simple, tasty and plentiful. A birthday? Cake and ice cream magically appeared. A special occasion called for a unique dish stealthily placed between the Costco baked chickens and vegetable medley.

This was Monday night at the Walker homestead—an old fashioned open table. In the world of Uber Eats and Lean Cuisine, a regular communal dinner seemed like a historical artifact of a bygone era. Not there. It was a center of gravity…Deb Walker dishing out hugs, kisses, greetings and a buffet of food. A reminder that Christian faith is often best experienced around a dinner table of people arriving as strangers and departing as friends.

Deb's passing called an old book off my library shelf this past week: *Loving Across Our Differences* by Gerald Sittser—a wonderful book about how groups of people can build community by moving beyond things that divide us. Sittser elevates the "commands of mutuality" we find in the New Testament. "One-another commands," he calls them. "Greet one another," "Forbear one another," "Encourage one another," and "Serve one another," "Comfort one another," "Bear one another's burdens," "Stir up one another," "Prayer for one another," "Love one another."

There's more. You can find them. Simple in concept, difficult in execution. Nobody understood their significance better than Deb.

If the foundational element of Christian behavior is love, says Sittser, how then do we practically love others? Great question. Sittser's answer: practice the "commands of mutuality." The totality of love is encompassed in them.

Day Thirty-Six: Open Table

I still desperately want to hit the reply button and thank Deb for her last encouraging email. But I keep thinking she'd demonstrate graceful forbearance and in her genteel southern drawl say, "Honey, where I am I've got all the encouragement I need! You go find someone who really needs that message and share with them."

Thanks Deb, that's what I'll try to do.

REFLECTIONS

> "Rituals also force a pause. Many wise people self-consciously divide their life into chapters, and they focus on the big question of what this chapter is for. Rituals encourage you to be more intentional about life. People can understand their lives' meaning only if they step out of their immediate moment and see what came before them and what they will leave behind when they are gone."
>
> "We've become pretty casual over the years. We've become reasonably present-oriented. As a result, we've shed old rituals without coming up with new ones. We've unwittingly robbed ourselves of a social architecture that marks and defines life's phases. We've robbed ourselves of opportunities to celebrate. Why do we willingly throw away chances to throw fun parties about important things?"[70]
>
> –David Brooks

WRITING THE BETTER STORY

1. Write about a "command of mutuality" that is difficult for you to practice. Write down a way you can practice that command within the next week.

2. Write about a "command of mutuality" that comes naturally for you.

3. What's a ritual you might add to your life—a ritual that will bring a deeper sense of meaning, purpose and joy?

DAY THIRTY-SEVEN
THANKSGIVING CALLS

"Real religion…is this. Look after orphans and widows in their distress…"
–James 1:27

"At this stage I think I'd rather die from loneliness," shared the 88-year-old voice on the other end of the phone. "I've not seen my family in 7 months. I'm just so…so tired of being alone." I was uncertain how to respond.

The past few weeks I'd been returning voicemails left on my mother's answering machine. News got out that she was recovering in the hospital from a recent fall, and her friends were checking for updates on her recovery. It was heartwarming to experience the concern of companions who spanned decades.

As someone spending 90% of his life thinking about issues impacting children and teens, I've found myself unexpectedly thrust into the world of octogenarians—female octogenarians more specifically. Allow me to make an observation—completely anecdotal—based on my recent conversations with Louis, Vernie, Pat, Nancy, Sheila, Marg, and Dorris. All widows. All living alone. All in their 80's and 90's:

Many of our elderly citizens are lonely and experiencing life-crushing social isolation. It's a problem. It's growing.

My octogenarian sensitization is pushing me to see beyond my normal social sphere of younger colleagues, active 50-something-year-old peers, and the friends of my young adult children. It's opened my eyes to the painstakingly long, empty days our seniors experience, shut off from social contact with family or friends.

"We're just lonely." That's the cry bubbling to the surface.

A few years ago, a friend shared a heartening story of his mother. She kept a list of names and numbers by her phone. Her husband of 60 years had recently passed away, so she'd often find herself a little melancholy at certain times of the day. "When I'm feeling a little blue," she confessed, "I pick up the phone, call someone who is worse off than me and try to encourage them. It makes me feel a better." Her story surfaced in my memory this week.

"Fundamentally we are social creatures and part of what brings meaning to our lives is to maintain and foster those social connections," Lisbeth Nielsen, from the Institute of Aging, reminds us. "Loneliness is the sense of suffering from being disconnected from other people."

Perhaps a special opportunity presents itself for those of us who own a phone. What if each of us makes a list of people we know who live alone—individuals whose social connections have been disrupted, who are sick, or in an assisted living facility? Once we've compiled our list, let's make a few phone calls and say hello, ask a few questions, express a word of gratitude or even say a prayer. Our listening ear and audible voice will be a welcome gift.

The apostle Paul, when writing to the church of Galatia, says: "Carry one another's burdens, and in this way, you will fulfill the Law of Christ." At this moment in history, loneliness certainly qualifies as a burden. Those of us blessed with the love of family and friends can carry a little burden for those whose wavering hearts pine for days of crowded kitchens and laughter around the supper table. A short phone call can fulfill the Law of Christ—and put a little Thanksgiving joy in someone's heart.

REFLECTION

"So many things we achieve are achieved only through struggle and conflict, not in easy ways. They always seem to involve crosses. I have so longed to find somewhere in life, some corner where joy is unmingled with pain. But I have never found it. Wherever I find joy, my own or other people's, it always seems to be mingled with pain. And I find that the people I most respect are people who know the link between joy and pain. And I have found that if we will own pain and weep over it together, we also find Christ's overflowing comfort. The bad news is that there may be no corner of reality where joy is not related to pain. The good news is that there is no corner of reality where pain cannot be transformed into overflowing joy."[71]

–John Goldingay

WRITING THE BETTER STORY

1. Make a list of people who might be lonely, sick, struggling, depressed, or experiencing some kind of loss. Call a few of them. Write a note.

2. Is there a moment when you experienced pain that eventually manifested itself in a form of joy? Write about the experience.

DAY THIRTY-EIGHT
ANGELS EAT GRANOLA BARS

*"You've made us—people—a little lower than angels.
You've crowned us with glory and honor."*
–Psalm 8:5

"I'm hoping you can help," surged the opening line. "We have a situation that needs to be addressed urgently."

Quickly I scanned the rest of the email, trying to get to the heart of the issue, my curiosity piqued. There are situations and there are *situations*. Over the years I've learned some you can solve quickly with very little emotional energy. And there are those situations that drag on indefinitely and can never be resolved.

"One of our 12-year-old girls," revealed the email's Malawian author, "is being offered to an older man for a dowry."

To westerners the concept of dowry is foreign. Our society has definitely benefited from the women's movement and civil rights. The idea of a young woman, offered to an older man for some kind of financial compensation, is an affront to sensibilities and our values. Yet in a culture where parents or guardians cannot afford to feed and educate their daughters, the dowry system is an opportunity to alleviate a burden.

"How much is the dowry?" I replied, waiting for the return email, wondering if this was going to break our ministry budget.

What I didn't realize is that many young girls are still being offered up for a dowry in sub-Sahara Africa before the age of 17. Even more tragic than having 12-year-old girl married off to a 40-year-old man is that these girls often become nothing more than domestic slaves who are subject to abuse and ridicule of the man. Educational aspirations are thwarted, confining these young women to lives of poverty.

Dyna was one of those girls. Orphaned by her parents, an elderly grandmother took her in. But the expense was too great to bear. A marriage proposal seemed like a good option. An attendee in our after-school program in a small village of Kanunga, just outside of Malawi's capital city, our staff begged the grandmother to reconsider. But they would need resources to negotiate.

"A chicken and a goat," came the reply in my inbox. "And we need to guarantee that we'll provide her school fees and feed her once a day."

"What's the U.S. equivalent of a chicken and goat?" I countered, hitting send with a sense of urgency.

"Thirty-eight dollars," was the reply, minutes later.

Thirty-eight dollars? *What?* Thirty-eight dollars was the barrier between a young girl pursuing her dream of furthering her education and a life of indentured servitude. I could feel myself getting a little hot under the collar. At that moment I remember thinking about my two daughters pursuing their university education, growing as human beings and becoming independent. *Life is so unfair.* At that moment I remember asking myself if I really believed that every human being is "just a little lower than the angels."

I needed to act. This was a situation that could easily be solved.

I wrote to my friends and shared the story. Guess what? $38 checks arrived in the mail—in abundance. I've got amazing friends. Not only were we able to help Dyna, but we were able to start a campaign to help girls who were vulnerable to the dowry system.

Day Thirty-Eight: Angels Eat Granola Bars

Six months later, I had the opportunity to travel to Malawi with a few of my friends who helped with the dowry campaign. They wanted to meet the girls they had sponsored.

I'll never forget introducing my board member, Rebecca, to the young woman she sponsored—a girl named Mathia. Rebecca, a PhD Chemist, and a passionate advocate for girls, met Mathia at the edge of her village. Mathia wanted to show her sponsor where she lived.

Before starting the journey down the path toward her hut, Rebecca pulled a granola bar from her pocket, unwrapped it, broke it in two and gave half to her new little friend. As Rebecca consumed her piece of the bar, she failed to notice that Mathia buried her piece in her pocket. They began to walk and talk.

Arriving at the red mud, grass roof hut, Rebecca surveyed the situation: no running water, no electricity, no toilet, no concrete floor, no beds. Just mud walls. A dirt floor. Flies. And a little wooden stool for Rebecca to sit upon as their honored guest. A disorienting moment—a situation unlike anything Rebecca had experienced.

Out of the corner of her eye, Rebecca noticed Mathia dip a hand in her pocket and pull out her piece of granola bar. Mathia broke it in half, gave half to her little brother who, in turn, broke his piece in half and gave it to his smaller sister. Everyone received a small piece.

"I couldn't believe my eyes," recounted Rebecca that night. "In the midst of abject poverty, Mathia displayed the most profound act of generosity I'd ever seen. I realized, at that moment, I was in the presence of an angel."

REFLECTION

"It helps, now and then, to step back and take the long view. The kingdom is not only beyond our efforts, it is beyond our vision. We accomplish in our lifetime only a tiny fraction of the magnificent enterprise that is God's work... We cannot do everything and there is a sense of liberation in realizing that. This enables us to do *something* and do it very well. It may be incomplete, but it is a beginning, a step along the way, an opportunity for God's grace to enter and do the rest. We may never see the end results, but that is the difference between the master builder and the worker. We are workers, not master builders, ministers, not messiahs. We are prophets of a future not our own."[72]

—Bishop Ken Untener

WRITING THE BETTER STORY

1. What's one small action you can do today to add another paragraph to your story? Write about it.

2. Write about someone you can look at differently this week—what would it mean to view them as someone "just a little lower than the angels?"

DAY THIRTY-NINE
SHE SAID YES

"...let it be to me according to your word."
–Luke 1:38

"A text popped up on my phone," shared Sio. "It was 7:30pm and I was just settling down for a quiet evening."

Our leadership team had been discussing the meaning of Advent when Sio asked to share. Leaders spoke about the need to use Advent as a time to open our hearts to the promptings of God. Some discussed the Advent tension between patience, preparing, waiting and expecting. Others talked about how Advent is a lifestyle—slowing down enough to create a posture of making ourselves available to God. Something in the discussion prompted Sio to speak up.

"The timing of the text was inconvenient, but I felt compelled to respond," she continued. "So, I stepped out of the family room to find a private place to talk and dialed the number. On the other end was a distraught young man who used to attend our programs."

Fortunately, Sio has a degree in social work and is a gifted crisis counselor. For the next hour, she persuaded the young man to not engage in an action he would regret for a lifetime—an act with serious consequences. She asked him questions, walking through different scenarios and prioritizing what he valued most in his life. "I really want to be there for my child," he finally confessed as the call concluded, "I want to be a good dad." Sio glanced at her watch. Family time would have to wait until tomorrow.

The next day the young man called Sio again. "Thank you," he shared, choking back tears. "My son called me this morning. If I had followed my instincts last night, I would have missed the chance to talk with him. He needed me."

"I hesitated to respond to that call," Sio admitted to our leaders. "I knew this wasn't going to be an easy conversation, but I was reminded that God needs us to make ourselves available, even when it's inconvenient. I'm glad I said yes because God always writes a better story than we can ever imagine."

As I listened to Sio's story, my thoughts raced to the Christmas story—especially the moment when Mary said yes to God.

"I am the Lord's servant," announced Mary, after learning she'd been chosen to miraculously mother Jesus. "Let it be to me according to your word" (Luke 1:38). These words are Mary's invitation for God to create something beautiful through her. God never forces. God never coerces. God simply announces the opportunity. A divine invitation extended: we have a choice to say "No" or "Yes."

When Mary says *yes*, the dynamic, mysterious and miraculous possibilities of God are birthed through her. When Mary says, "let it be to me," she yields to God's bigger story, even though God's request is improbable…surprising…and yes, inconvenient. Christmas begins with a perplexed teenage girl basically saying, "I'm a little freaked out by the visiting angels and I'm not really not sure how I'm supposed to conceive a child as a virgin…but I'm willing to trust, lay my fears and doubts aside, and say yes."

Our Franciscan friend Richard Rohr echoes when he writes, "There is no mention of any moral worthiness, achievement, or preparedness in Mary, only humble trust and surrender. She gives us all, therefore, a bottomless hope in our own little state."

Sio said yes to an inconvenient phone call and God's good news envelopes a distraught young man. A teacher says *yes* to God by search-

Day Thirty-Nine: She Said Yes

ing for a child who has missed two days of online learning—only to discover his family can't pay the electric bill and needs assistance. A church group says yes to God by creating Christmas and Easter goodie bags for our teachers, affirming their value and worth. All around me people are saying *yes* to God—and the light of Christ shines.

Let us not forget that the God of Christmas is the same God who chooses to birth the miraculous through ordinary people who simply say…YES.

REFLECTION

> "So, when the coronavirus came, I thought, 'I'm a miracle. I will make it. I have to make it.' During the war, we didn't know if we would make it a day. I didn't have any freedom. I couldn't speak loudly, I couldn't laugh, I couldn't cry. But now, I can feel freedom. I stay by the window and look out. The first thing I do in the morning is look out and see the world. I am alive. I have food. I go out, I go for walks, I do some shopping. And I remember: No one wants to kill me…I still sometimes feel that I am missing out. A full year is gone. I lost my childhood, I never had my teenage years. And now, in my old age, this is shortening my life by a year. I don't have many years left…I understand the fear people have, and I understand you have to take care. But there is no comparison of anxiety, of the coronavirus, to the terror I felt when I was a child. That was fear with no boundary. This is going to end, and I am already thinking, planning where I am going first, what I will do first, when this ends."[73]
>
> —Toby Levy

"The apostle James well described the difference between faith and empty faith. Dead faith bears no fruit, shows no evidence of transformation. The criterion to judge faith is the quality of the believer's life as a living witness...not a mere assent to doctrine and creed."
—Jim Wallis, *Agenda for Biblical People*

WRITING THE BETTER STORY

1. Life is short and there are no guarantees. Why wait to say *yes* to God? What prevents you from saying yes to God?

2. Write about a time you said yes to God. What happened? How did you see God at work?

DAY FORTY
FLOWERS IN BARREN PLACES

"I will make cedar trees grow in the desert...."
–Isaiah 41:19

"Here's how my faith has grown this past year," shared our young leader during morning devotions. He paused a few seconds, furled his eyebrows, and continued: "I feel like a tree in the winter. Leaves are gone—fallen to the ground. The tree looks dead. Barren. Lifeless. Yet inside it's still very much alive. In winter dormancy the cells prepare for rebirth with those first warm rays of spring sunshine. That's me. Stripped down, but not dead. God is still at work."

Our program staff listened intently. All could relate to some degree. It had been a year of losing our leaves—even branches for some of us. The word *barren* aptly described our situation.

"An interesting choice of metaphor," I countered. "Especially around this Christmas season."

"What do you mean?" queried the young man.

"Well, Christmas trees are the exact opposite of what you described," I began. "We bring them into our houses green. We decorate them with lights and ornaments. Water them. They look very much alive and beautiful, but they're really dying."

Interesting contrast. Two trees. One looks dead but is very much alive. One looks very much alive, but it's actually dead. An alien from another planet—not knowing anything about the seasonal cycles of trees—might choose the shiny lights and tinsel as the tree with a probable future. J.R.R. Tolkien's words ring true: "All that glitters is not gold."

The Christmas story centers around two very improbable situations. I find it fascinating. One is a pregnancy involving an older woman, a barren womb and the unplanned birth of a prophet named John the Baptist—a man who eventually brings a searing critique to a broken and dead religious system. The other is a pregnancy involving an ordinary teenager—who's had no relations with a man—who births a child who brings light, hope and redemption to the world. Both are highly improbable situations.

"I am an old man and my wife is well along in years," laughed Zechariah to the angel Gabriel (Luke 1:18). Reading between the lines: "In case you've not noticed, Gabe, my wife and I have aged out on the kid thing—we're way too old to be thinking about babies!"

Yet this is the irony of the Christmas story—it's a story built around the unlikely and improbable. For the cynic and skeptic, the whole story is a problem—a stumbling block on the path to belief. Yet those willing to imagine with faith, that improbability only bolsters our hope, especially as we confront the impossible and barren realities of our own circumstances.

Consider the following as well: The Christ does not come from a prestigious and noteworthy city. He hails from a backwater town called Bethlehem. The Christ is not born to a politically connected or wealthy family. His parents were peasant teenagers who couldn't even afford a decent place to stay. The Christ did not enter the world through a well-oiled religious system. He came as an unscheduled gift of God, who operates beyond the limitations of human control and design. Nothing about the Christmas story really makes sense on a logical level. It's beauty coming from the barren.

Day Forty: Flowers in Barren Places

A little like the crowds of people who made the 258-mile trek from Los Angeles to Death Valley, California a year ago this April. They came to witness the improbable: an unusual desert phenomenon called the Super Bloom. In the hottest, most arid, most life-adverse place on earth a rare spectacle of colorful flowers carpeted the desert floors in oranges, yellows, and pinks for a few glorious days. A week earlier there was nothing but sand, rocks and a little tumbleweed filling the landscape. Yet freak winter rains activated the dormant life below the surface. Beauty from the barren.

That's certainly the UrbanPromise story as well. It's why I still believe in the potential of trees that look barren, deserts that look arid and forgotten places nobody notices. Its why I believe Christmas is so much more than turkey, football, gift exchanges and carol singing. Christmas is the improbable story that's been changing the world for the past 2,000 years.

Thirty-seven years ago, a barren, dying Baptist church in East Camden became a "manger" for a new movement of God's work. With a few faithful volunteers, lots of prayer, scarce resources and a handful of trusting kids, the improbable happened. Three decades later: schools and summer camps, boatbuilding and community gardens, jobs for teens and streams of Camden's young people growing into their God-given potential. And to everyone's surprise, UrbanPromise has now spread to 40 locations around the world—populating overlooked and under-resourced communities, reaching thousands of vulnerable children every day in Trenton, Wilmington, Charlotte, Nashville, Little Rock, Miami, Toronto, Vancouver, Honduras, Kenya, Malawi, Nigeria, Columbia, Liberia, Ottawa, Uganda, Mexico, Ghana…that's improbable. A Super Bloom.

So for those of us feeling like we've lost some leaves and luster this year, or maybe our Christmas lights have short-circuited—prize ornaments have crashed to the floor—remember it's in the barren places, the broken places, the improbable places that the God of Christmas is very much alive and working. That's good news. That's joy for the World.

REFLECTION

"Jesus loves you too much to fulfill your expectations and dreams. That's because he has his own dreams for you that are greater than anything you have imagined."
—Craig Barnes

"It isn't just Lazarus who is in the tomb. It is you and me. We entered that tomb the day we gave up on life, the day we gave up adventure for security and settled for life without passion, risk, or a clear sense of mission....We entered the tomb the day we said, 'That's the way it is and you can't change it.'"[74]
—Craig Barnes

WRITING THE BETTER STORY

1. Do you feel your dream for your life is too limiting? Is there a dream, vision or mission that you've been repressing? If so, write about it.

2. What is a barren situation God has placed on your heart? What might it look like to engage that situation with hope and the promise of God's life-transforming power?

ENDNOTES

1. Angel Kyodo Williams, forward to Valerie Mason-John, Detox Your Heart: Meditations for Healing Emotional Trauma, rev. ed. (Somerville, MA: Wisdom Publications, 2017), ix, x.
2. Meredith Dodd, A Palestinian Boy, an Israeli Soldier and my American Sons, Christian Century, September 27th, 2017
3. Ilia Delio, "Falling Inward, Falling Upward: God, Self, and the Liberation of Love," Oneing 11, no. 2, Falling Upward (Fall 2023): 49-50
4. Sara Miles, Interview Church Times, July 28th, 2010
5. Tomas Halik, Night of the Confessor: Christian Faith in An Age of Uncertainty (New York: Image, 2012), 55
6. Richard Rohr, Faith and Belief: Weekly Summary, Saturday, July 22, 2017
7. Rabbi Jonathan Sacks, Lessons in Leadership: A Weekly Reading of the Jewish Bible (Jerusalem, Israel: Maggid Press, 2015), 22
8. William Sloan Coffin, Credo (Louisville, KY: Westminster John Knox Press, 2004),7
9. Mike Nicol, Mandela: The Authorized Portrait (Kansas City, Missouri: Andrews McMeel Publishing, 2006), 7
10. Cynthia Bourgeault, The Wisdom Way of Knowing (Old Saybrook, Connecticut, Tantor Media, 2020)
11. Fr. Greg Boyle, Barking to the Choir: The Power of Radical Kinship (New York: Simon & Schuster,2017), 134
12. The Presbyterian Outlook, An Easter Tribute to William Sloane Coffin in his own words, April 25, 2006
13. Fr. Greg Boyle, Tattoos on the Heart: The Power of Boundless Compassion, (New York: Free Press, 2010),
14. Dietrich Bonhoffer spoke these words in a sermon January 15th, 1933 called, Overcoming Fear. The sermon was based on Matthew 8:23-27. It was a time of great tension and fear in Berlin.
15. Henri Nouwen, Lifesigns: Intimacy, Fecundity and Ecstasy in Christian Perspective (New York: Image Book, 1986),11

16. Amanda Barratt, The White Rose Resists: A Novel of the German Students Who Defied Hitler (Grand Rapids, MI: Kregel Publications, 2020), 24

17. Ann Weems, Lament 5 from "Psalms of Lament," (Louisville, KY: Westminster John Knox Press, 1995)

18. Elie Wiesel, U.S. News and World Report 27, October 1986

19. Walter Brueggemann, The Costly Loss of Lament, (JSOT, 1986), 57-71

20. Seyward Darby, White Supremacy Was Her World. And Then She Left, New York Times, July 17, 2020

21. John Stifler quotes Boyce in an article called, A Partnership in Haiti, Christian Century Magazine, January 2, 2019

22. Pope Francis, The Name of God is Mercy Treatise: General Audience Talks on God's Mercy, Edited by: Bartholomew C. Okonkwo (Raleigh, NC: Lulu Press, 2016), 73

23. Ed Simon, In Praise of Wonder, New York Times, December 14th, 2018

24. Kent Keith, Anyway: The Paradoxical Commandments, (Maui, Hawaii: Inner Ocean Publishing, 2001)

25. Robert E. Quinn, Deep Change: Discovering the Leader Within (San Francisco: Jossey-Bass, 1996), 35

26. Randy Pausch, The Last Lecture (New York: Hachette Books, 2008)

27. David Brooks, The Moral Bucket List, New York Times, April 11, 2015

28. Priest Responds to Gang Member' 'Lethal Absence of Hope' with Jobs, and Love, NPR, November 13, 2017

29. Desmond Tutu with Douglas Abrams, God Has A Dream: A Vision of Hope for Our Time (New York: Image Books/Doubleday, 2005), 19-22

30. Pope Francis, 109

31. Sean Litton, Abolitionism at the Tipping Point, (Interview by Andy Olson), Christianity Today, Jan/Feb 2019, 76

32. Quote from MLKing Jr, "I have a Dream" Speech, August 28, 1963. My summary does not do Dr. King's sermon justice. You can read in its entirety here and be challenged and encouraged by its fullness https://kinginstitute.stanford.edu/king-papers/documents/draft-chapter-x-shattered-dreams

33. William Hutchinson Murray, The Scottish Himalayan Expedition, 1951

34. John Tierney & Roy Baumeister, For the New Year, Say No to Negativity, Wall Street Journal, December 27th, 2029

35. Parker Palmer, The Active Life: A Spirituality of Work, Creativity, and Caring (Hoboken, NJ: Jossey-Bass, 1999), 17.

36. C.S. Lewis, The Four Loves (New York, HarperCollins, 2002)

37. As quoted by Charles Duhigg, Wealthy, Successful and Miserable, New York Times Magazine, February 19th, 2019

38. Ezra Klein, George Saunders: "What I regret most in my life are failures in kindness," Washington Post, August 4th, 2013

39. Zadie Smith, The New School 2014 Commencement, (www.newschool.edu/commencement)

40. Thomas Merton, 'The Merton Prayer' from Thoughts in Solitude (The Abbey of Our Lady of Gethsemani, 1956)

41. Paul Sloan, Leading with Questions, March 8th, 2018 (leadingwithquestions.com)

42. Public Affairs, Berkeley News, Googles Eric Schmidt to Graduates: Find a way to say yes to things, May 14, 2012

43. David Brooks, The Second Mountain: The Quest for a Moral Life (New York: Random House, 2020)

44. Emily Esfahani Smith, On Coronavirus Lockdown? Look for Meaning, Not Happiness, New York Times, April 7th, 2022

45. Richard Leider, The Power of Purpose: Creating Meaning in Your Life and Work (Berrett-Koehler Publishers, 2005),p 8

46. Leider, p 8

47. Victor E. Frankl, The Unheard Cry for Meaning (New York: Simon & Schuster, 1978)

48. Margaret Wheatley, Leadership and the New Science (San Francisco, CA: Berret-Koehler,2006), 20

49. Amy Ziettlow, A Spot for Lent (Psalm 121; John 3:1-17), The Christian Century, March 6, 2020

50. Liam Stack, Stirring Sermons About Coronavirus, in Empty Cathedrals, New York Times, March 15th, 2020

51. Max Lucado, When God Whispers Your Name (Waco, TX: Word, 1994)

52. Robert C. Morris, Enlightening Annoyances: Jesus' Teachings as a Spur to Spiritual Growth, Weavings, XVI, Number 5
53. Father Michael Doyle shared this truth with me before he died in 2022. I've not forgotten.
54. Thomas Merton, "Love and Need" in Love and Living. Naomi Burton Stone and Brother Patrick Hart, editors. (New York: Farrar, Straus & Giroux, 1979), 30-31
55. Brene Brown, The Gifts of Imperfection: Let Go of Who You think You're Supposed to Be and Embrace Who You Are(Danvers, MA, Hazelden, 2010)
56. Cynthia Bourgeault, The Wisdom Way of Knowing: Reclaiming Ancient Tradition to Awaken the Heart,(Hoboken, NJ: Jossey-Bass, 2003) 74-75
57. The Acorn Parable was originally created by Maurice Nicoll in the 1950s.
58. Richard Rohr, The Art of Letting Go: Living the Wisdom of Saint Francis (CD)
59. Brennan Manning, Abba's Child: The Cry of the Heart for Intimate Belonging (Colorado Springs, CO: NavPress, 1994)
60. The O Magazine, October 2009, What I know for Sure, p. 232
61. Brennan Manning, Abba's Child: The Cry of the Heart for Intimate Belonging (Colorado Springs, CO: Nav Press, 1994)
62. Henri Nouwan, Sabbatical Journey: The Final Year (New York: Doubleday, 1992), 127
63. Dorothee Soelle, Death by Bread Alone (Minneapolis, Minnesota: Fortress Press, 1978)
64. Frederick Buechner, Beyond Words (New York: HarperOne, 2004)
65. Cynthia Bourgeault, The Meaning of Mary Magdalene: Discovering the Woman at the Heart of Christianity (Boulder, Colorado: Shambhala Publications, 2010), 8,15-16
66. Rollo May, The Courage to Create, (New York: WW Norton & Company,1994),12
67. Henri Nouwan, "Intimacy, Fecundity, Ecstacy," Radix (May/June, 1984), 8-23
68. Marianne Williamson, A Return to Love: Reflections on the Principles of A Course in Miracles (New York: HarperOne, 1996)

69. Thomas Merton, The Climate of Monastic Prayer (Collegeville, Minnesota: Liturgical Press, 2018) 52-23

70. David Brooks, There Should Be More Rituals, New York Times, April 22, 2019

71. John Goldingay, Walk On: Life, Loss, Trust, and Other Realities (Grand Rapids, Michigan: Baker Books, 2002)

72. This prayer was first presented by Cardinal Dearden in 1979. It is an excerpt from a homily written for Cardinal Dearden by then-Fr. Ken Untene for the mass of the deceased priests, October 25th, 1979 aptly titled, "Prophets of a Future Not Our Own."

73. Toby Levy, The Holocaust Stole My Youth. Covid-19 is Stealing My Last Years, New York Times, 1/3/2021

74. Craig Barnes shared this homily with the UrbanPromise staff when he was president of Princeton Theological Seminary. These were quotes constructed from his presentation.